How Long Things Live

Anthony D. Fredericks

STACKPOLE BOOKS

0 11557 03622 0

To Jack and Linda Sommer –
for all the grins, giggles, and guffaws!

Copyright © 2010 by Stackpole Books

Published by
STACKPOLE BOOKS
5067 Ritter Road
Mechanicsburg, PA 17055
www.stackpolebooks.com

Printed in the United States

10 9 8 7 6 5 4 3 2 1

First edition

Library of Congress Cataloging-in-Publication Data

Fredericks, Anthony D.
  How long things live / Anthony D. Fredericks. — 1st ed.
      p. cm.
  ISBN 978-0-8117-3622-0
  1. Life spans (Biology) 2. Longevity. I. Title.
  QH528.5.F74 2010
  570—dc22
                                    2009047913

INTRODUCTION

The way I see it, getting old is a lot like being on an airplane. Someone is always telling you something you've heard before. You have to squeeze into spaces the human body was not designed to occupy. And it's a constant challenge keeping things in their fully locked and upright position.

We have a fascination with age and getting old. Turn on the TV, listen to the radio, or pick up a magazine or newspaper and you will be bombarded with products (often pitched by charlatans) that promise a youthful appearance—wrinkle-free skin, a full head of hair, slim body, tighter tush, muscular physique. Age, it seems, is something to be feared or eliminated. Youth is something to admire and maintain. Wisdom doesn't come with age, it comes with selecting the best cosmetics, medical products, Botox injections, and diets to turn us back into something we once were, or think we once were.

Since the dawn of civilization, humans have been fascinated with age. True, our earliest ancestors didn't have many years to look forward to. The life expectancy of the average Neanderthal was probably fewer than 30 years—hardly enough time to get a stock portfolio in place, set up a college fund, or save for a down payment on a condo. Nevertheless, humans have historically been consumed with thoughts of age. Many cultures revere and celebrate it; others fear it.

In fact, humans have been more obsessed with age—more specifically, with longevity—than perhaps any other concept. We're consumed by the notion of a fountain of youth. We've embraced the story of Methuselah, who supposedly lived to the ripe old age of 969. We've searched for a mythical Shangri-La—a village where everyone lives well into their third century (picture a group of 273-year-olds sipping mint juleps in deck chairs). We succumbed to a crafty salesman named P. T. Barnum, who deftly separated Americans from the contents of their wallets by promoting (among other things) a 161-year-old woman who was actually a spry 80-year-old with a great hairdresser. We even celebrated the 50th birthday of Barbie . . . yes, Barbie, the doll! Suffice it to say, humans in general, and Americans in particular, have an obsession with longevity. Not only do we want to live forever, we want to do it looking like we did at our senior prom.

We continue to be fascinated (and in some cases duped) by cases of people who lived well past normal expectations. In its various editions throughout the 1960s, '70s, and '80s, no less an authority than the *Guinness Book of World Records* stated, "No single subject is more obscured by vanity, deceit, falsehood, and deliberate fraud than the extremes of human longevity." Over the years, numerous stories, claims, and "scientific experts" (also known as publicity agents) have surfaced claiming various Confederate soldiers, Appalachian mountain people, and Caribbean hermits living to be 297, 185, and 125 years old. (Which raises an interesting question: What do you get a 185-year-old for his birthday? Depends.)

If given the chance, statisticians at the National Center for Health Statistics will trot out charts and graphs to show how most United States citizens can expect a life span (depending on heredity and lifestyle) of somewhere around 75.2 years for men and 80.4 years for women. (Scientists typically define "life span" as the period of time between the birth and death of a life form—this span of time will, quite naturally, vary from species to species, and from individual to individual, as it does from human being to human being.)

For example, your typical worker ant (depending on the species) can expect to live for a brief, if very hectic, 45 to 60 days. At the opposite end of the scale, a newborn Galapagos tortoise can expect a full and rich life (sunbathing and eating juicy succulents) of up to 200 years.

Life spans are, at best, averages. They are estimations and approximations of how long a typical individual or entire species will live. A chicken can expect an average life span of about 8 years—just enough time to raise a couple broods, peck around the yard, and add an appropriate amount of droppings to the nutritional content of the soil before going off to that great chicken coop in the sky. Yet there have been chickens that have lived well into their teens, which would be the upper extreme of the creature's life span.

Recently, a group of scientists determined that among mammals there may be a correlation between brain size and longevity. That is to say, the larger a mammal's brain, the longer it is expected to live. In other words, large cetaceans (aquatic marine mammals) always have longer average life spans than do small insectivores. So if you are planning to be reincarnated, you might want to think "fin whale" instead of "pygmy white-toothed shrew."

But the extremes of species' life spans fascinate us most. Extremes defy averages, challenge the status quo, and give us all something to shoot for. If humans are expected to live until 85 and one of us lives to 110, that's exciting. If domesticated cats have an expected life of 12 years and Fluffy lives to be 24, that's exciting. If the average life expectancy of a hippopotamus is 30 years and one lives to be 55, that's exciting.

In this book, I included average life spans as well as the extremes—the upper limit of a plant or animal's existence. To record those limits, I had to look at a wide range of information. As you might expect, whenever we begin talking about "upper limits" we are subject to interpretation, exaggeration, and perhaps fibbing. I tried to make all the entries in this book as accurate as possible. To do so, I consulted a plethora of scientific reports and chatted with numerous zoologists, botanists, and other investigators to be sure that what is recorded here is scientifically sound. Some records were obtained from zoos, some from scientific papers and scientists, some from face-to-face interviews, and some from verifiable documentation.

I am well aware that there is, and will always be, room for error. Not everyone adheres to the same set of scientific standards or protocol. The folks working at a zoo, for example, who observe (and feed and care for) a particular animal on a daily basis may record their information differently than does a scientist who performs an autopsy on a specimen. A dendrologist may estimate the age of an ancient tree using one set of criteria while a paleobotanist might use an entirely different set of standards.

That's not to say that one method of record-keeping is better than another, only that each might be subject to slightly different interpretations. In all cases, the data reported here have been double-checked, thus providing the most accurate and up-to-date information possible. I am sure there will be those who will challenge the accuracy of some of these records. They, like me, will undoubtedly discover conflicting data, disparate analyses, and varying degrees of accuracy throughout a wide range of documents. So it is in the world of biology—total agreement is sometimes transitory and may frequently be contested. Should scientific discoveries or accounts change over time (or I transform myself into a larger mammalian species with the accompanying increase in cranial function), the records will be corrected in future editions.

Unlike most biology textbooks that present plants and animals in a hierarchical format, from the simplest (protozoa) to the most complex (humans), here they are ranked by the extremes of their life spans—shortest to longest. We start with a creature whose entire life takes place in less time than it takes to drink a double latte at Starbucks and end with one that has been in existence since long before we humans descended from primates and simplified our lives with BlackBerrys. In between are some of the most amazing, fascinating, intriguing organisms ever to grace this planet. This order puts us humans in our rightful and proper place among all living things—right in the middle.

MAYFLY

5 minutes

I suppose that if you knew you had a very short time to live there would be no better way to spend that time than to produce a batch of kids to carry on the family tradition after you're gone. Most animals don't get to make that choice—it's decided for them by Mother Nature.

In your search for the creatures with the shortest life spans you need look no further than the insects, which represent the largest group of animals in the world. In fact, the folks at the Smithsonian Institution estimate that there are some 10 quintillion (that's 10 with 18 zeros) individual insects alive today, which works out to more than 1.47 billion insects for each human on the planet. Scientists have also calculated that the world holds 300 pounds of insects for every 1 pound of human.

Entomologist Craig Welsh, of the University of Florida, is one of a hardy band of scientists who spend their lives studying critters most of us would rather not see, much less talk about. Welsh and his colleagues are consumed by the life expectancies—specifically, the *short* life expectancies—of select species of insects. He notes that many insects spend the majority of their lives in the immature stages of development (most insects go through four stages of growth: egg, larva, pupa, and adult). Although there are several species among many groups of insects that exist for only a few days as adults, the record so far for the briefest reproductive life of any creature on earth belongs to the female American sand burrowing mayfly (*Dolania americana*).

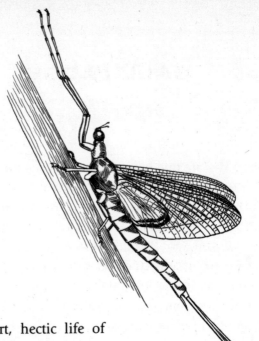

The short, hectic life of
this creature takes place in less
time than it does for you to read the
front page of your daily paper or eat a
Big Mac. After its final molt, and in just
about 5 minutes, the female of this species
must locate a suitable mate, copulate, and then
return to its watery origins to lay a clutch of eggs.
Then it dies. Its entire life is dedicated to one and only
one function: preservation of the species.

This sand burrowing mayfly is a member of an order of
insects known as Ephemeroptera—the word *ephemeral* (meaning short-lived) is derived from the origin of this name. Most
of the members of this group live for fewer than 48 hours—a
time span so short that they don't have time to eat. In fact,
almost every member of this order lacks functional mouthparts. As a result, they are unable to consume any type of nourishment during their fleeting (yet highly intense) lives.

GALL MIDGE
3 hours

Midges are tiny insects found throughout North America and Europe. Perhaps the most notorious are the biting midges—summertime pests along the Atlantic seaboard often referred to as "no-see-ums." Their extremely small size (less than ¼ inch long) is responsible for their nickname, and their irritating (I mean *really* irritating) bite is far out of proportion to their size.

There are more than 3,300 species of gall midges—tiny, fragile insects. They are economically significant—in a negative way—because of the extensive damage they do to wheat, alfalfa, pears, blueberries, raspberries, and other crops. Gall midges attack plants and trees, creating what are called galls, distinct swellings of plant tissue. The galls develop in leaf bud tissue and often adversely affect the productivity of the plant by interrupting normal growth and reducing vigor and flowering ability. (There is one species of midge that attacks mosquitoes, "stealing" the blood the mosquito has just sucked from another animal—it's an actual mosquito pest.)

Another species of gall midge—*Rhopalomyia tripleurospermi*—discovered in Slovakia in 1972 and since found in eastern Austria, northern Hungary, southern Moravia, and parts of western Canada, has one of the shortest known life spans of the gall midge family. Males and females of this species are for the most part distinctly different. Males have long wings, dark brown heads, gray abdomens, and long, slender legs. Females, which contain fully developed eggs, are larger than the males in proportion to how many eggs they are carrying. They sport a bright red abdomen and shorter legs.

The females deposit an average of ninety-three bright red eggs into leaf axils or flower buds, individually or in clusters of two to seven. Adult *R. tripleurospermi* emerge from the top of galls in the previous year's buds during the spring when temperatures remain above 46°F for 125 days. Adult females live for only 12 hours at 77°. Males, at that same temperature, have a considerably shorter life span—just 3 hours, or 180 minutes.

PINE PROCESSIONARY MOTH

24 hours

As is the case with all moths, the pine processionary moth starts out as a caterpillar—in this case, one that cuts a distinctive figure, with an orange-brown back and bluish-gray bands and protrusions, each of which sports clumps of hair. It is these hairs that can be a significant gastronomic problem for creatures who like to put creepy-crawly things in their mouths. The hairs contain a highly allergenic protein, which in humans can cause reactions ranging from mild itching all the way up to full-blown anaphylactic shock. Animals that ingest these creatures often experience necrosis of the tongue, resulting in severe, often deadly, breathing difficulties.

The pine processionary moth lays its eggs in the summer. After hatching, the young caterpillars congregate in the upper branches of pine trees to form enormous nests, each composed of colonies of several hundred individuals. These congregations not only provide safe haven for the caterpillars, they also create a mini-environment several degrees warmer than the surrounding temperature. This helps ensure the survival of these creatures over the cold winter months.

In the spring, the caterpillars leave the safety of their colonies and travel down to the ground in order to pupate. To do this, they form long nose-to-tail "circus elephant lines" or processions (hence the name) as they make their way down the tree trunks and into the soil. This is one of the few species of caterpillars that actually makes physical contact with other caterpillars as they wend their way toward the ground. Many other species form similar conga lines but avoid actual contact.

When the adult pine processionary moth emerges from the soil in the summer it must go about its business quickly, for it will be dead by the next morning. Its sole purpose, as you might expect, is to find a potential mate, copulate, and lay eggs, after which it dies. The moth's total life covers about one complete rotation of the earth on its axis.

HESSIAN FLY

48 hours

The life cycle of a Hessian fly is, as they say, short and sweet . . . very short and sweet. This persistent pest of wheat farmers across North America was most likely brought to the continent in the late 1700s, probably in straw bedding from the southern Caucasus region of Russia. Since most of these flies were "imported" during the Revolutionary War, they were given the name Hessian in reference to the German mercenaries who fought against the colonists. These days, the pest can be found from Nebraska to the Atlantic Ocean, from Maine to Georgia, and in a few isolated areas of the Rocky Mountains.

In the Midwest, the Hessian fly is one of the most destructive of wheat pests. Fall-infested wheat usually dies during the winter, while spring-infested wheat produces grain that is typically unusable. Damn those flies!

In the northern parts of the country, the Hessian fly completes two generations per year; in the South, as many as six generations per year have been reported. Eggs are deposited in and around wheat plants, with maggots hatching in 3 to 7 days. The maggots crawl down into the leaves and feed at the plant's crown or joints. They then metamorphose over a period of 25 to 30 days into the pupa or "flaxseed stage" of development. The pupae have brown heads and white bodies with a reddish tinge. At this point in their life cycle, the creatures have grown from about 0.02 inch (as an egg) to as much as 0.24 inch (as a pupa).

Some time later, the actual flies emerge from their flaxseed stage, mate, deposit their eggs on the wheat, and die—all in about 48 hours. The second generation of maggots emerges and begins the cycle all over again.

GASTROTRICH

3 days

Like most folks, I enjoy a three-day weekend—those extended by a national holiday or some other celebration to last longer than the usual Saturday-Sunday pairing. But there's one creature for which the three-day weekend is not just something to celebrate—it's an entire life span. Consider the gastrotrich, a microscopic creature (0.002 to 0.12 inch long) frequently found in both fresh and saltwater environments. It is so small that marine species are able to wiggle their way between the zillions of sand particles that make up a beach. The name comes from the Greek words for stomach *(gaster)* and hair *(thrix)*. I don't know about you, but being referred to as a "stomach hair" might cause me to crawl between some sand grains, too.

There are nearly 750 species of gastrotriches throughout the world, including 100 species in North America. They are well dispersed in tropical, subtropical, and temperate waters worldwide. According to some scientists, they are frequently regarded as the most abundant but least well-known freshwater invertebrate. In some freshwater environments, they may be found in densities of a million per square yard.

The gastrotrich's body is covered by cilia, and it moves by waving these tiny hairs back and forth. Two of the most interesting features of these creatures are the terminal projections at one end of their bodies. Each of these projections is tipped with a special gland—one that secretes a glue to help the creature adhere to a surface, the other that secretes a de-adhesive to sever the connection when the critter wants to move.

Most species of gastrotriches are hermaphroditic—they have both male and female reproductive organs. This means that any one gastrotrich can mate with any other gastrotrich. At least one source reports that the creatures might also be proterandic hermaphrodites—males early in life, then changing into females. To further muddy the sexual waters, some species have reduced testes, while at least one species has lost its left testis. Other species of gastrotriches reproduce via parthenogenesis, which is reproduction without fertilization.

The creatures come in handy. Scientists believe that marine species of gastrotriches may help decontaminate coastal areas by consuming debris washed ashore, thus preventing its decay and resultant odor. Gastrotriches typically feed on diatoms, bacteria, and minute protists. Not much of a diet, but they have to plan meals for only 3 days.

HOUSE FLY
25 days

"Live fast, die young!" might be the motto of this much-cursed creature. The average life span of an adult house fly *(Musca domestica)* is 15 to 25 days. In fact, flies can complete their life cycle (egg, larva, pupa, adult) in as few as 7 to 10 days. Active only during daylight, especially during summer picnics, they spend the night in dark, protected places.

House flies go through a process known as complete metamorphosis. A female fly will lay about five hundred eggs in several batches of approximately seventy-five to one hundred each. After about 1 day, larvae (what you and I call maggots) hatch from the eggs. The larvae feed on dead and decaying organic material and live for about 1 week, then crawl to a cool, dry place to transform into pupae. Adult flies emerge from the pupae and live for another 2 weeks to a month. At this point in the life cycle, flies cease to grow.

Flies have been around for a long time. Although the order of flies (Diptera) is much older, true house flies evolved in the beginning of the Cenozoic era, 65.5 million years ago. Their worldwide dispersal is probably due to their co-migration with people (thanks a lot, fellow humans).

House flies have despicable table manners. Because they cannot eat solid material, when they come upon a likely food source, they spit saliva on it to do some predigesting, after which they suck it all up. They will also regurgitate partly digested matter and pass it again to the abdomen.

Because they eat a lot, house flies deposit feces constantly, which is one of the factors that make the insect a notorious disease spreader. Flies are capable of carrying over a hundred pathogens, including typhoid, cholera, salmonella, dysentery, tuberculosis, anthrax, and parasitic worms. Health organizations around the world fight a never-ending battle to curtail the transmission of fly-spread diseases.

The California Institute of Technology recently conducted some interesting studies on flies. They found that a fly anticipates the approach of a threat (your hand sweeping down to crush it, for example) and is thus able to alter its stance to make the most effective getaway. This highly evolved evasive reaction allows the fly to jump in about 200 milliseconds, considerably quicker than the blink of an eye.

Two more fascinating fly facts: They can walk up walls or across ceilings because of the surface tension of liquids secreted by glands on their feet. And when they are not flying, flies spend considerable time preening, cleaning their eyes with their forelegs and dusting off their legs by rubbing them together.

One more fact: Some biologists have calculated that, under optimal conditions, a single pair of house flies beginning reproduction in April would produce 191,010,000,000,000,000,000 offspring by August.

CORAL REEF PYGMY GOBY

59 days

Imagine the disappointment the African turquoise killifish must have felt when it learned that it was no longer the world's shortest-lived vertebrate. There it was, peacefully living its brief, 24-week life in the waters of equatorial Africa, when a pair of Australian scientists swimming around the Great Barrier Reef's Lizard Island happened upon a tiny reef fish that lives, as Australians are fond of saying, "flat out like a lizard drinking."

The fish they discovered was the coral reef pygmy goby (*Eviota sigillata*), a tiny critter about ½ inch long that is one of seventy species of goby found along Pacific and Indian Ocean reefs. The scientists were researching cryptic coral reef fish, those that hide or camouflage themselves, when they came upon one of the smallest of all reef inhabitants.

But it wasn't the size or appearance of the fish that amazed the scientists—it was its incredibly short life span. Research on the goby's ear stones, known as otoliths, revealed the fish's secrets. Otoliths are calcium structures in fish ears (yes, fish have ears) that, like the human inner ear, help maintain balance. The otoliths accumulate layers of deposits similar to the rings of an onion. In gobies, a new ring is laid down every day, so all the scientists had to do was count the number of rings to arrive at the maximum age of the fish, which was an astonishing 59 days.

Additional research revealed the goby's brief reproductive cycle. With a reproductive window of just 25 days, the female pygmy goby is able to lay three clutches of eggs, totaling about four hundred. Once the eggs are laid, the male goby stands guard and fans the eggs to provide them with oxygen. After hatching, the minute goby larvae leave the reef for the open ocean, where they live for about 3 weeks (assuming they aren't consumed by bigger fish). Afterwards, they settle on the coral reef, where they mature for 10 more days before mating and starting the whole process all over again.

It has been speculated that the goby's rapid growth and maturation come as compensation for its reduced life span. Researchers postulate that small reef fish like the pygmy goby may be under constant stress from larger predators (in fact, daily mortality rates of 2 to 8 percent of the entire population are quite common). This may have led to severe biological time constraints and intense selective pressure for some species to evolve brief but very productive life spans. One scientist has stated that this discovery underscores the diversity and complexity of the coral reef ecosystem, which features a variety of evolutionary extremes.

MOSQUITO
100 days

Mosquito means "little fly" in Spanish (although many of us would translate the word as "damned pest" or, more accurately, "#*&%@* pest"). There are approximately 3,200 recognized species of mosquitoes throughout the world (approximately 150 occur in North America), but it's interesting to note that not *all* mosquitoes are bloodsuckers. And among those species that do suck blood, only the female does the sucking. That's because she needs the protein found in blood to produce eggs. Males of those species, as in most species of mosquitoes, spend a majority of their lives sucking fruit juice.

Mosquitoes are found pretty much everywhere, from deep in the Arctic to vast, sun-drenched deserts. The majority of mosquito species, however, prefer the warm, damp conditions normally found in temperate or tropical regions. Most mosquitoes need water—in a puddle, river, stream, lake, or abandoned tire—in which to lay their eggs. Two to three days after laying, the eggs hatch into larvae, called "wigglers," that feed on minute plants and animals in the water. It is only when they change into adults that they search out other food sources (such as you or me).

Bloodsucking females locate potential victims through an elaborate set of sensory receptors known as palpi, located at the ends of tiny feelers. These organs pick up traces of carbon dioxide gas and lactic acid, which is constantly excreted through sweat glands. Mosquitoes use these scents to determine whether an animal has blood or not; the sensors are so accurate that a mosquito can detect an animal's breath or sweat from a distance of more than 50 feet.

When a mosquito (again, only the females) locates a potential blood source, it lands on the skin and begins to poke its proboscis into a blood vessel near the surface. The proboscis, similar to a very sharp needle, is formed by interlocking mouthparts that quickly and painlessly penetrate the outer skin. Once it locates blood, the mosquito injects saliva into the wound to prevent clotting. The itch you get when a mosquito "bites" is an allergic reaction to the saliva (those maddening, red bumps are not really bites at all).

Mosquitoes are vectors—organisms that carry diseases from one animal to another. Mosquitoes are dangerous not because of their bites but because of the germs in their saliva, some of which can cause serious disease or even death in other animals. Some of the most serious and life-threatening diseases in the world—such as malaria, yellow fever, and dengue—are transmitted by mosquitoes.

As an example that nature sometimes seems to favor females much more than males, female mosquitoes can live for up to 100 days. Males, on the other hand, live for only 20 days. So much for the life-extending benefits of fresh fruit.

HONEY BEE
120 days

Busy as a bee? You bet! The short life of a worker bee is filled with chores and responsibilities—not only for herself, but for the survival of her entire colony. (That's right: The females do all the work in a honey bee colony. The males, known as drones, live a much shorter life, about 25 days, and exist for only one purpose: to mate with the queen.)

Honey bees go through four distinct stages during their short lives: egg, larva, pupa and adult—a complete metamorphosis. To start the cycle, the queen bee lays a single egg in each cell of a honeycomb (which is, of course, built entirely by females). By the fourth day, the egg hatches into a larva, which resembles a tiny white worm and is fed a special diet called beebread, a mixture of pollen and nectar. On the ninth day, the honeycomb cell is capped with wax, and the larva begins transforming into a pupa. The pupa stays entombed in the cell and doesn't eat for nearly 3 weeks. At about the twenty-first day, the new adult worker bee emerges from the cell and instinctively knows all the work she has to do, which she diligently accomplishes for 1 to 4 months until she dies. Female honey bees have sole responsibility for finding pollen and nectar, from which honey is made. (Bees do not actually create honey; they just improve upon the plant's nectar.)

Bees are essential to the growth of many crops. It's been estimated that nearly a third of the human food supply depends on insect pollination, principally by bees. To make one pound of honey, workers in a hive fly fifty-five thousand miles and tap up to two million flowers. In a single collecting trip, a worker will visit between fifty and one hundred flowers. She will return to the hive carrying more than half her weight in pollen and nectar. Despite all this heavy lifting, a single bee will produce only a fraction of a teaspoon of honey.

There are more than twenty thousand known species of bees throughout the world. Most researchers believe the honey bee originated in Africa. Since then, it has been found on every continent except Antarctica and in almost every environment in which there are flowering plants. It's been around for a while—one recently discovered extinct species dates from the Cretaceous Period, some hundred million years ago.

Scientific analysis by researchers at Cal Tech has determined that a honey bee is capable of flapping its wings approximately 230 times per second, which works out to nearly 14,000 beats a minute. Even with all this flapping, however, bees can only travel at an average speed of about 15 mph.

It's interesting to note that bees are one of the very few insects used for commercial purposes (think of Honey Nut Cheerios, Honey Maid graham crackers, Sue Bee honey, even Nasonex allergy medication). It seems marketing people are reluctant to use a cockroach or maggot as a spokesperson.

CHAMELEON

16 weeks

I'd like to now ask you to slip into the nearest bathroom, stand in front of the mirror, and stick out your tongue. If you're like most people, your tongue is probably 3 or 4 inches long, and you use it to help you talk and eat and taste your food (and signal displeasure with someone you'd rather not be with). Now imagine if your tongue were as long as your entire body and you could extend and retract it in less time than it takes to snap your fingers. You must admit this would be an incredible ability—particularly when trying to liven up a dull meeting.

There's one amazing animal—the chameleon—that has not only this wonderful talent but also another skill, one for which it is perhaps better known. In fact, when most people think about animals that are able to camouflage themselves, chameleons come to mind. This second ability, however, is slightly misunderstood: It's a misconception that chameleons can change their body color to match their surroundings—that the color of their skin can be altered to resemble a branch, leaf, or other colored surface on which they are resting. In reality, as biologists tell us, chameleons don't look at what's around them and then change their skin color to match it.

Different species of chameleons (there are about 171 throughout the world) have groups of colors or patterns they are able to display. Some of these colors are appropriate for camouflage, others not. A chameleon's skin color changes in response to the intensity of sunlight, the temperature of the air, the surrounding humidity, or even the animal's emotional state. It also has the ability to let other chameleons know how it feels, especially during mating season. If a chameleon loses a fight with another chameleon, its skin will turn dark green. If it's angry, the skin will change to black.

A popular attraction at zoos, chameleons range in size from the enormous malagasy giant chameleon (27 inches long) to the diminutive *Brookesia* chameleon (about 1 inch long). Although many species live 10 years or so, there is one unlucky species—the Labord's chameleon *(Furcifer labordi)*—that has a life span considerably shorter. This unusual reptile develops inside an egg for up to 9 months. Upon hatching, it lives for about 4 months, during which it rapidly matures, mates, and dies. Hatchlings emerge sometime in November and reach sexual maturity in January. By the beginning of February, however, they begin to show signs of old age, often falling out of trees because of a weakened grip. Soon after, the forest floor is littered with their bodies. Researchers from the American Museum of Natural History have remarked that this life cycle is more similar to those of insects than to those of reptiles.

One of the most distinctive features of all chameleons is their eyes, each of which can move independently. Swiveling its eyes up or down allows the chameleon to observe two separate objects at the same time or look at the same target from different angles. This ability is particularly handy when the chameleon searches for food.

Chameleons typically prey on insects, spiders, scorpions, and other small invertebrates. Some of the larger species will attack small birds, mammals, and lizards. The chameleon is a very patient hunter. When it locates a potential meal, it will observe it for some time before attacking. Its attack, however, is quick. Its tongue shoots out, catching the victim on the tip and carrying it back into the chameleon's mouth. Powerful muscles and a specially shaped bone in the chameleon's mouth contribute to the quickness of this action.

Using high-speed video and x-ray film, Dutch biologists calculated that the chameleon's tongue shoots out of its mouth at more than 26 body-lengths per second. This works out to be about 13.4 mph, considerably faster than most of us can run. They also calculated that the chameleon's tongue shoots out to 20 feet in about 20 milliseconds—faster than the acceleration of a jet fighter. In other words, if a chameleon stuck its tongue out at you, you'd probably never know it.

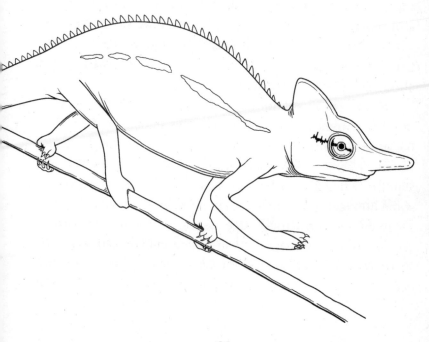

TURQUOISE KILLIFISH
24 weeks

Popular as aquarium fish, killifish are found throughout the world, primarily in the Americas, Europe, Africa, and Asia. Most live in permanent streams, rivers, and lakes and have an average life span of between 2 and 3 years. There are approximately 1,270 different species, ranging in size from 1 inch to just under 6 inches. All killifish are oviparous (meaning egg-laying) and are often found in large, free-swimming schools that include at least one dominant (and very territorial) male.

Killifish feed primarily on aquatic arthropods—insect larvae, tiny crustaceans, and worms. Some species eat plankton, and a few are carnivorous and eat mainly other fish. The golden wonder, a popular killifish often found in pet stores, is distinctive because it has a mouth that's as wide as its head, allowing it to eat other fish its own size.

One of the most famous of all killifish is the Devil's Hole pupfish *(Cyprinodon diabolis)*, listed as endangered in 1967 because its only known natural habitat is in the 93-degree waters of Devil's Hole Cavern, in the Ash Meadows National Wildlife Refuge in Nye County, Nevada. Although the cavern is some 400 feet deep, the pupfish are believed to spawn exclusively on a shallow rock ledge just below the water's surface. The population of these pupfish has never exceeded 553 since surveys began in 1972. Over the years, the number has continued to decline for reasons unknown: An April 2006 count indicated an adult population of only 38 individuals, the lowest count on record.

Another killifish species that is piquing the interest of biologists worldwide is the turquoise killifish *(Nothobranchius furzeri),* a freshwater species found in Mozambique and Zimbabwe. This fish typically inhabits ephemeral ponds in semiarid regions with scarce and erratic precipitation. It has adapted to the frequent drying of its environment by evolving desiccation-resistant eggs that can remain dormant in dry mud for several years, a process known as *diapauses,* a physiological state of dormancy (similar, I believe, to the state children achieve when they are asked to do household chores).

Because the rainy season in east Africa is relatively short, the life span of the turquoise killifish is limited to just a few months, typically between 12 and 24 weeks. It is during this short existence that the fish hatches, matures, reproduces, and dies. Because of its abbreviated life span, the killifish has become a valuable research tool in studies of animal aging. Scientists at the Fritz Lipmann Institute in Germany, for example, are currently studying the genetic and molecular mechanisms that influence the accelerated aging process of this unusual species.

LEAF INSECT

1 year

Here's an insect that is practically unnoticeable simply because it looks like a leaf. This extraordinary creature—known as the leaf insect—resembles vegetation so closely that it is almost indiscernible, an immense help in escaping detection from predators, even when viewed up close. And since leaves are everywhere in the insect world, this characteristic has helped ensure the leaf insect's survival.

Young leaf insects are usually marked and colored like glossy, green leaves, including branched vein patterns similar to those on a living leaf. Occasionally, they have a couple of brown spots that mimic marks left on leaves by disease or the nibbling of other critters. The limbs of leaf insects also resemble leaf parts—the legs and head are often shaped like flat extensions of a leaf. When aware of an approaching predator, leaf insects remain motionless for several hours to complete the disguise.

Generally, leaf insects rely on color to avoid predation, but some species use active defense mechanisms. For example, a few have large spines on their legs. By rapidly bringing their legs together, these creatures can inflict a painful wound on a would-be attacker. Other species are capable of making a loud, hissing noise with their wings or have brightly colored wings that they flash to startle predators. A number of species can produce a defensive spray capable of causing temporary blindness and a great deal of discomfort to humans as well as other creatures.

There are thirty-six species of leaf insects throughout the world. Most inhabit forests and woodlands, principally in tropical regions. Many can be found in Australia and Southeast Asia. They live, on average, 1 year.

BEDBUG

18 months

Like tax collectors and poor customer service, bedbugs have been around since ancient times. They live in temperate climates throughout the world and are uniquely adapted to human environments, especially the creases and crevices of bedding material. Adult bedbugs are reddish-brown, flattened, oval, and wingless, about ⅛ inch long, the size of an apple seed.

Bedbugs are generally active only at dawn, although they sometimes feed at other times. They are attracted to warmth and the presence of carbon dioxide. As soon as a bedbug locates a suitable target (you sleeping, for example), it jabs the host with two hollow tubes. With one tube, it injects saliva, which contains anticoagulants and anesthetics; with the other, it withdraws blood. After feeding for about 5 minutes, the bug returns to its hiding place. A bedbug can consume five times its body weight in a single feeding. A dermatological reaction to the injected agents results in the itching experienced by the host some time later.

Determining the life expectancy of a bedbug is tricky business. Well-fed bedbugs—those that obtain blood every 5 to 10 days—will live for an average of 9 to 10 months. However, these creatures also have the capacity to go into a state of dormancy when they aren't able to obtain a ready supply of blood. Ironically, without a dependable food source, they may survive for up to 550 days, or almost 18 months. In other words, they can live longer without food than with it.

While there is a common misconception that bedbugs are associated with filth, such is not the case. They are attracted not by dirt but by exhaled carbon dioxide and body heat. In short, they feed on their hosts, not on waste. (It is their cousin the cockroach that has an affinity for unsanitary living conditions.)

Besides the feeding behavior, another bedbug habit might give you pause. The critters mate via a process known as traumatic insemination. Instead of inserting its genitalia into a female's reproductive tract, a male bedbug pierces a female with hypodermic genitalia and ejaculates directly into the body cavity. This form of mating is thought to have evolved as a way for males to overcome female resistance.

SQUID

2 years

The fastest a human can swim the Olympic 50-meter freestyle is about 5.25 mph. A squid can swim almost five times faster, up to 25 mph, and do it backwards. The nerves in a squid can carry impulses at a rate of 50 mph (human nerve impulses travel 4.5 mph). As a result, squids can sense danger and zoom off in milliseconds—all of which does little to explain why so many wind up as appetizers (maybe *calamari* is Italian for "not quite fast enough").

A squid can outswim almost every other marine animal of its size. It's able to do this because its rocket-shaped body is perfectly suited for racing at high speeds. And the creature has powerful muscles that contract to force out a jet of water like a blast from a fire hose. Repeated blasts allow the squid to zigzag through the water in its quest for food. One species, the hooked squid, can even "fly"—taking off from the water, gliding in formation, zooming through the air like a flying fish, sometimes landing on the decks of ships at sea.

Squid can be found in every ocean of the world, from the depths of the Pacific Ocean to the shallow waters of the Atlantic and Indian oceans. Some species are quite large—the famous giant squid can reach a length of 42 feet and weigh just over 1 ton. Others are tiny: *Pickfordiateuthis pulchella* is about ³/₄ inch long and the favorite food of many fish and whales. Most of the three hundred species of squid, however, are no more than 24 inches long.

Like its cousin the octopus, a squid has eight arms covered with powerful suckers. It also has two tentacles, used to capture small fish, crabs, and other sea creatures. When a fish is caught, the squid kills it with a bite from its powerful beak. It then removes the head of the fish and strips the flesh from its bones. Hannibal Lector would be proud.

Squid are noted for their excellent eyesight, which is more advanced than any other invertebrate's. Not only does their eyesight help them locate food, it also identifies approaching enemies. (The giant squid has eyes the size of dinner plates.) When an enemy is sighted, squids protect themselves by emitting an inky fluid and escaping through the clouded water. As additional protection, some species can change their colors.

Squid live in a variety of habitats—from warm, tropical waters to colder regions. They are prized as a gastronomical delicacy throughout the world, however, and several species have been listed as endangered.

WALKING STICK

3 years

S top! Freeze! Sit perfectly still! Don't move a muscle! How long do you think you can hold that position? One minute? Five minutes? Thirty minutes? If you're like most people, you find it very difficult to stay motionless for any great length of time. But there is an amazing creature in your backyard or nearby forest that can remain motionless for many long hours. Not only can it stay perfectly still, its body shape and coloration make it look exactly like the twig or branch on which it rests. As a result, this creature—the walking stick—is almost invisible to a casual observer or a hungry predator looking for a meal.

Walking sticks are members of a family of insects called Phasmidae, a Greek word meaning apparition, ghost, or phantom. Indeed, these creatures might be the ghosts of the animal world. Extremely thin, with long, spindly legs and compressed bodies, they are green or brown and look exactly like a twig, stick, or plant stem. In fact, all their body parts resemble plant parts. When they walk, these curious creatures look like animated twigs; when they are still, they look like an extension of a tiny branch or a small stick.

Walking sticks are known by a variety of nicknames, including devil's riding horse, prairie alligator, stick bug, witch's horse, devil's darning needle, and (my favorite) musk mare. Some species occur in two different colors, brown and green. When exposed to excess humidity and darkness, a few species are able to turn dark; when normal humidity and daylight return, the dark color disappears.

The walking stick is common throughout the United States. Although it's hard to see in its natural environment, its eating habits can easily be detected. In fact, it's considered a pest in some parts of the country because it defoliates large tracts of trees.

Despite its clever camouflage, the walking stick is sometimes located by predators such as birds, midges, and wasps. If captured, it can break off one of its legs, thus leaving the attacker with only a very small morsel. It can regrow the lost limb over time.

Walking sticks are one of about three thousand species of stick insects that live throughout the world, mostly in tropical regions. They have completely lost the power of flight but have been able to adapt to their surroundings with a distinctive combination of physical traits.

BLACK WIDOW SPIDER

4 years

Black widow spiders might be some of the best-known creatures in the animal kingdom. Uncountable numbers of scary stories surround this tiny arachnid, turning it into an animal that is somewhat larger than life. These tales are so prevalent because black widows can be found throughout the warmer parts of the whole world. In the United States, they inhabit every state except Hawaii and Alaska.

Their most noteworthy physical feature is the red hourglass shape on the underside of their abdomens. They often build their webs in abandoned buildings, cellars, attics, and other cool, dark places. There they wait for flies and other insects to fly into their webs and get trapped.

Black widow spiders can be dangerous creatures, not only to the insects they capture and eat, but to humans as well. In humans, black widow bites can produce muscle aches, nausea, and paralysis of the diaphragm that can make breathing difficult. Bites can also be fatal, but usually only to small children, the elderly, or infirm. Fortunately, death is quite rare; the spiders are nonaggressive and bite only in self-defense, such as when someone accidentally brushes against them or sits on them. Even so, the venom of a black widow spider is fifteen times more potent than a rattlesnake's poison.

Female black widows sometimes eat the males after mating—hence the name. Many people believe that females always eat the males, but biologists have proved otherwise. Females only eat their mates when they are hungry (a paltry reassurance, I'm sure, for male spiders). In essence, the mating process is a perilous activity for the male black widow. He must play a guessing game, hoping that the female he approaches is well fed.

Not only are black widow spiders cannibalistic during mating, they are equally dangerous to each other after hatching. After mating, the female black widow lays up to a thousand eggs in an egg sac in the middle of her web. After a few days, the tiny spiderlings hatch and begin to scurry about. Unfortunately, they usually have nothing to eat but each other. So, until they are old enough to build their own webs, larger spiderlings often eat their smaller brothers and sisters. Typically, less than 25 percent of newborn black widow spiders survive to adulthood.

Most species of spiders have relatively short life spans, normally up to a year. Black widows, however, have a life span of between 1 and 3 years. In captivity, where their environment is controlled and they are less prone to cannibalistic behavior, black widow spiders can live for as long as 4 years.

MONGOLIAN GERBIL

8 years

Gerbils are one of the most popular small pets in the United States, and of the 110 species of gerbils in the world, the Mongolian gerbil is the one most often kept in American homes (more specifically, in preadolescent bedrooms). The creature was discovered in eastern Mongolia in 1897 and first imported into this country in 1954. Wild gerbils usually live in large burrows that extend underground and consist of several chambers for nesting and storing food. Although primarily herbivorous, gerbils will supplement their diet with insects and, on occasion, other gerbils.

Female gerbils give birth to several litters a year, with each litter consisting of one to nine babies. The birth takes place after about 3 weeks gestation, and the babies stay with the mother for another 3 weeks. It is not unusual, however, for the mother to attack and eat her offspring. This cannibalistic behavior occurs when the mother does not get enough protein in her diet. The easiest way for her to supplement this deficiency is by eating her young. As a result, the babies' protein and other nutrients are recycled back into the mother's body.

Overcrowding can also lead to one of two other forms of cannibalistic behavior. One occurs when there is more than one mother in the nest at the same time. If one mother's litter is left unguarded, her babies might be killed and eaten by the mother of another litter. Another form occurs when there is insufficient food available. In these cases, a mother might kill and eat one litter while protecting and defending a previous litter.

As with many other animals, the average life span of gerbils varies widely and is often dependent on where they live. For example, the average life span of a gerbil in the wild is less than 6 months. Gerbils in a laboratory setting, however, can live for an extended period of time—one captive laboratory specimen lived for 6.3 years. Several pet websites describe gerbils living for up to 8 years in captivity. Presumably, these long-lived gerbils did not have to socialize with gerbils who were prone to intraspecies snacking.

SEA CUCUMBER

10 years

The sea cucumber looks like something that grows in your garden or along the side of a country road. But it's actually an animal. Sea cucumbers are members of a group of animals known as echinoderms, or spiny-skinned animals. Other members of this group include sea urchins, starfish, brittle stars, and feather stars. All echinoderms live on the ocean floor, never in a garden.

There are more than fourteen thousand different species of sea cucumbers throughout the world. The smallest is 0.6 inch long; the largest grows to a length of about 3 feet. Sea cucumbers typically have leathery, warty bodies shaped (of course) like cucumbers and rows of tube feet on their flat undersides. They use their feet to drag themselves along the sea bottom.

At one end of the sea cucumber is its mouth, which is surrounded by several tentacles. Most sea cucumbers ingest mud, small plants or animals, and plankton. Some burrowing sea cucumbers swallow sand as they plough through it, digesting the edible matter it contains and eliminating the rest. Studies of sea cucumbers living on coral reefs have shown that there may be up to two thousand to the acre, passing nearly 60 tons of sand through their bodies each year. In fact, much of the sand around some coral reefs has at one time passed through the body of a sea cucumber. (One study in the San Juan Archipelago in Washington found 1,618,400 sea cucumbers per acre. We can only guess how much sand they've eaten.)

At the other end of the sea cucumber is an anus, which, for this creature, serves two purposes: discharging body waste and breathing. Most sea cucumbers breathe by pulling water through their anuses and into the body cavity. There it mixes with body fluids to supply the creature with oxygen. In some species, the anus also provides shelter for a tiny fish known as a pearlfish, which is small enough to slip into the sea cucumber's anal opening. There it hides from predators with just its head sticking out.

The primary enemies of sea cucumbers are starfish and certain types of bottom-dwelling fish. The sea cucumber has a most unusual method of defending itself from these predators. If it's threatened, it discharges its internal organs—they are shot out from the anus and, depending on the size of the predator, completely envelop it or stick to its sides. The surprised predator usually swims off while the sea cucumber burrows into the sand or escapes beneath a rock. There it spends the next few days regrowing a completely new set of organs.

In the Far East and South Pacific, sea cucumbers are considered delicacies; they are grown, harvested, and used for food. They are eaten raw or dried and used to make soup. Sea cucumbers fortunate enough to escape a fisherman may live for 10 years. Those that end up in a cooking pot are often considerably younger.

KRILL

11 years

In the Antarctic Ocean, pods of whales eat millions upon millions of tiny sea creatures, all in one gulp. And it's not necessarily the whales that are most interesting but the animals they eat: krill.

Krill are small shrimplike creatures that live in some of the coldest waters on the planet. With a pair of large, black eyes, an elongated cephalothorax with modified limbs, and five pairs of paddlelike appendages on a 2-inch body, an individual krill looks like an alien being from a distant world, or a guitar player in a grunge-rock band.

What is so amazing about these crustaceans is their enormous numbers: Uncountable congregations swim through the icy waters of Antarctica. These groups might be as small as a few feet across or more than an acre in size—a whirling mass of billions of organisms swimming together, assuming circular, oval, or oblong shapes. Krill are pink, and so the assemblages can turn large portions of the ocean's surface pink. At night, krill are luminescent—they light up and become a colossal mass of blue-green fire surging through the sea.

When threatened, at least one species of krill—*Euphausia supera*—will literally jump out of its shell, hoping, most likely, that a chasing predator will go after the shell, giving the tiny creature a chance to escape.

Besides whales, krill are also a favorite food of seals, penguins, seabirds, and fish. In fact, many biologists believe that krill are the most important link in the entire Antarctic food chain—their sheer number makes them a readily available food source for a wide variety of animals.

Krill are now being considered as a potential food for humans, too. Because krill are high in protein, low in fat, and readily abundant, several nations are developing plans to harvest the tiny creatures. The danger is that wildlife that subsists almost entirely on krill might lose an important food source. By feeding humans, we could be removing an essential food from the table of other animals, putting them in danger of extinction.

HUMMINGBIRD

12 years

H old your arms out to the sides of your body. Now move them up and down as quickly as you can. How fast can you flap your "wings"? Twenty times a minute? Forty times? Although hummingbirds are one of the smallest birds in the animal kingdom, they are one of the most amazing—simply because of what they can do with their wings. (You can stop flapping now.) Some hummingbirds, such as the male ruby-throated hummingbird, found throughout much of North America, can flap their wings seventy to almost eighty beats *per second* (female rubythroats average about fifty beats a second).

Aided by this flapping, hummingbirds can perform incredible aerial maneuvers. Because their wings can swivel in all directions from the shoulder, they can fly forward and backwards (the only birds able to do this), up and down, and side to side. They can also hover like helicopters, remaining stationary in the air except for their beating wings.

The breast muscles of a hummingbird make up about 25 percent of its total body weight (our breast muscles, for comparison, constitute about 5 percent). Hummingbird hearts, which are larger in proportion to their bodies than are any other bird's, beat at a rate of six hundred times a minute during rest—and up to twelve hundred times a minute during exertion.

There are approximately 329 species of hummingbirds in the world. Although they range from southern Alaska to the tip of Argentina, most species are found in the rain forests of South America. Only about 16 species migrate to North America. The smallest hummingbird species, the bee hummingbird of Cuba, is less than 2 inches long; the largest, the giant hummingbird of Ecuador, Chile, Argentina, and Bolivia, is about 8 inches long.

Because they expend so much energy, hummingbirds require *lots* of food. In fact, they must feed an average of at least once every ten minutes. Despite what some people believe, hummingbirds do not use their tongues like straws to suck nectar from flowers or feeders. Instead, the forked tongue is grooved and laps up nectar about three times per second. Hummingbirds also eat insects, which provide needed protein and fat.

Although hummingbirds have been known to live for up to 12 years, the average life span is 3 to 5 years. The greatest loss of life for migrating species comes during their grueling twice-yearly journeys. Many species are also suffering from excessive loss of habitat, either in their summer or winter ranges, or both.

MOOSE

15 years

No doubt about it, a moose looks like it was assembled from leftover parts. It has a short tail like a deer, a beard like a turkey, ears like a burro, legs like a horse, shoulder humps like a bear, and a four-chambered stomach like a cow. It seems to have been designed by committee.

Moose belong to a group of animals known as ungulates, hooved animals that include elk, caribou, whitetail deer, and reindeer. The moose is, in fact, the largest member of the deer family. All ungulates are even-toed, with two large toes and two small ones.

The word *moose* comes from the Algonquin Indians, who once lived throughout the northern regions of Canada. They called this strange-looking creature *mooswa*, meaning "the animal that strips bark off trees." Early explorers gradually transformed it into our present-day name. For the Algonquins, especially during long and harsh winters, the moose was a most important animal—sort of a walking general store. The hide was used to make clothing and provide shelter. Bones and antlers were shaped into useful tools. And the meat was a dietary staple.

Zoologists estimate that a single moose needs between 1 and 15 square miles of forest or pastureland to survive. If there is plenty of food in a particular area, moose will stay there. It is not unusual for a moose to live its whole life within a 10-mile radius. If the food supply runs out, however, moose move to other locations to obtain what they need—on average, a moose needs about 40 pounds of food a day. The life expectancy of a moose is between 15 and 25 years, with 25 being at the extreme end of the range.

The coat of a moose is made up of "guard hairs" that can measure up to 10 inches long. These hairs are hollow, and the air trapped inside is warmed by the moose's body to insulate the animal in cold weather. The hollow hair also helps the moose float when it swims across a lake or pond. With its powerful legs, a moose can swim at a speed of about 6 mph. Believe it or not, that's faster than Michael Phelps. Moose have been observed swimming nonstop for distances of up to 12 miles.

If you're really into moose, you'll want to stop by Talkeetna, Alaska, in late June for the annual Moose Dropping Festival. Besides vendors, music, a softball tournament, and food stands, there's the not-to-be-missed Moose Dropping Drop. According to the chamber of commerce's description of this event, "shellacked and numbered moose poop is hauled up in the air in a net and then dropped on a bullseye. Raffle numbers correspond to numbers on moose poop. Winners include the closest and farthest from the bullseye." Sounds like fun.

CHICKEN

16 years

Most chickenologists will tell you that the maximum life span of an average chicken is about 7 to 8 years. That is unless the chicken is raised by a company called Perdue, in which case its life expectancy is about 8 weeks. But let's not think about the creatures that end up on barbeque grills and rotisseries. Instead, let's concentrate on those lucky enough to grow old with grace and dignity.

Considering that chickens are one of the most ubiquitous of all animal species—there are more chickens than people in the world, some seven billion fowl—it would seem difficult to identify the single chicken that has lived the longest. But the folks at the *Guinness Book of World Records* have come up with a champion: Matilda, formerly of Bessemer, Alabama, owned by Keith and Donna Barton. In April 2004, the Bartons gathered the necessary paperwork, and, after substantial review, Matilda was proclaimed to be the World's Oldest Living Chicken. She then went on tour, appearing with Jay Leno on *The Tonight Show* and strutting her stuff at several charity events. She was also the star of Keith and Donna's traveling magic show for several years.

Alas, the end came on February 11, 2006, when Matilda passed on. As of this writing, she still holds the record for fowl longevity—a full 16 years—and has been enshrined in the Alabama Animal Hall of Fame.

But in our discussion of chicken longevity I would be remiss if I did not include the story of Mike the Headless

Chicken. This distinguished fowl, formerly of Fruita, Colorado, literally lost his head on September 10, 1945, due to a misplaced swing of his owner's ax. Incredibly, this tough bird lived for 18 more months—without his head! Like Matilda, he toured the country and was featured in *Time* and *Life* magazines. At the height of his fame, he earned 4,500 dollars a month.

Since his passing, Mike has assumed cult status in Fruita. Every May, the town marks his death with a Mike the Headless Chicken Festival, which includes a car show, a 5K foot race, a chicken-dance contest, and, of course, all the fried chicken you can eat.

TICK

18 years

Biologists estimate there are about 850 species of ticks in the world. Most fall into two groups: soft ticks and hard ticks. The difference is determined by the hardness of their outer bodies, or exoskeletons.

Ticks exhibit a variety of life spans, too. In one laboratory experiment, an unfed adult *Ornithodoros lahorensis* tick lived for 18 years, and it seems safe to assume that this is the absolute maximum life expectancy for any species of tick. Another tick species, *Ornithodoros canestrinii*, has survived for 10 years in a laboratory setting, also without food. It is speculated that this tick's life cycle may extend to 16 years because of the cold temperatures and scarcity of hosts where they live, in Turkmenistan. By contrast, the common North American tick *Ornithodoros coriaceus* has a life span of only 3 to 5 years.

Ticks cannot fly; they can only crawl. After hatching, a tick crawls up a twig or blade of grass and waits for a host to pass by (this is known as questing behavior). During that time, the tick often desiccates, or dries up, and so must periodically descend to the leaf litter to rehydrate (a brief period in a tick's life known as quiescence). A tick may go back and forth between questing and quiescence several times before it locates a suitable host. It can survive without food for up to several months.

Ticks have very poor eyesight. They can, however, easily detect other animals in their presence. They are extremely sensitive to carbon dioxide, which all mammals exhale. When a questing tick gets a whiff of carbon dioxide, it instantly becomes activated, even if it has not moved for a long time. The tick leaps on whatever breathing animal is passing by. A wandering deer, for example, might be attacked by dozens of blood-sucking hitchhikers in a matter of minutes.

As soon as a tick lands on a host, it scuttles beneath the fur or hair and buries its mouthparts into the skin. The host does not feel a thing as the tick injects both an anesthetic and an anticoagulant. The tick feeds on the victim's blood for several days, even weeks. As it feeds, the tick's body swells up to many times its normal size. Eventually, it is so full of blood that it cannot drink any more. At that point, it loosens its head from the victim and falls to the ground.

Ticks are dangerous, not because they are bloodsuckers but because they are vectors—organisms that carry diseases from one animal to another. Ticks do this by drinking blood from an infected animal and then drinking from a healthy one. The infected animal's bacteria and viruses (which thrive in the tick's gut) are then quite efficiently passed along.

SCALLOP
19 years

Scallops are part of a group of animals called bivalves, meaning animals with two shells. Varying in size from 1 to 8 inches, scallops can be found throughout the oceans of the world. Their shells, covered with ridges and corrugations, are pink, red, or yellow. The symmetrical waves on the shell is where we get the term "scalloped," which refers to a way fabrics and potatoes can be cut.

The life span of scallops varies widely. Ever-popular bay scallops (those typically dripping with butter in seafood restaurants) have a well-defined life span of between 18 to 22 months, unless, of course, they wind up in a fisherman's net. The Florida Bay scallop, a favorite Southern delicacy, lives for about 1 year before dying off naturally or getting eaten by crabs, octopuses, or shell-crushing finfish. At the other end of the scale, the giant scallop is reported to live for up to 19 years. These creatures can be found in the western North Atlantic from the Gulf of St. Lawrence to the coast of northern Maine.

Some of the most distinguishing features of a scallop are the rows of tiny eyes along the edge of its mantle. Depending on the species, scallops may have up to 111 eyes, and each of these has a lens, iris, cornea, and double retina. One layer of retinal cells receives a focused image while the other responds to light intensity. Scallops have the ability to replace eyes lost through injury—in fact, a scallop can lose all of its eyes and re-grow them within 40 days.

There are approximately four hundred different species of scallops. They typically lie on the seabed with their shells open. Since they prefer shallow water, their shells are often washed up on shore, particularly after severe storms. Scallops have the ability to zip through the water like jet-propelled submarines. To do this, they open their shells and fill the interior space with water. Then the powerful muscle inside quickly contracts, pulling the valves shut and shooting water out behind. By doing this repeatedly, a scallop can move backward or forward with a side-to-side progression.

Most bivalves have two muscles, but the scallop has only one, and it is this single muscle that is so beloved by gourmands the world over.

SCORPION

25 years

Although the scorpion is one of the most feared of all desert creatures, only a fraction of the 1,520 different species of scorpions are dangerous to humans. In fact, scientists have found only about 50 species that are known to produce venom that can cause difficulties for people; of these, only a few are potentially lethal. Oddly enough, it's the small scorpions—the ones about 1 inch long—that are most dangerous.

Scorpions are related to crabs and lobsters. Scientists refer to these creatures as "living fossils" because they look very much like their ancestors did 395 million years ago. Most species are found in the warmer regions of the world. In the United States, they thrive in desert areas and have been found as far north as Oregon. They are primarily nocturnal animals; during the day, they hide under logs or rocks. The smallest scorpion in the world is only 0.2 inch long; the largest is 7.9 inches long.

Most species of scorpions have an average life expectancy of between 3 and 8 years. There are a few species, however, that can live for a maximum of 25 years. Unfortunately, there have been very few life span studies done on scorpions. Even so, biologists have been able to determine specific factors that influence their longevity. These include temperature, access to food, and whether the scorpion lives in the wild or in captivity (like many animals, scorpions tend to live longer in captivity). Some studies show that reproduction plays a significant role in the longevity of scorpions—mated individuals tend to die younger than virgins do.

Scorpions have poor vision even though some species have as many as twelve eyes. Because they hunt primarily at night, scorpions rely on other senses to locate prey. In some cases, a scorpion will walk around with its claws spread apart until it bumps into a spider or insect. More often, however, scorpions sense ground vibrations caused by prey walking nearby. The vibrations are picked up by sensory organs on the scorpion's legs as well as by special hairs on its body. When a victim is located, the scorpion's claws snap shut to trap the prey in a viselike grip. The victim is then torn to pieces or crushed. Afterwards, the scorpion sucks up the body juices.

If the prey is large or puts up resistance, the scorpion may use its stinger. Although it's not used as often as some people believe, that doesn't mean that it's not dangerous. A scorpion's stinger is lightning fast and lethally accurate against small prey. The stinger is actually a hollow tube connected to a poison gland near the end of the scorpion's tail. Muscles force the stinger into the body of the prey. Then poison is squeezed from the gland into the victim. The poison is usually powerful enough to immobilize or kill almost any struggling creature.

The scorpions that can be fatal to humans (particularly to children) have venom that acts on the brain as well as the body. Profuse sweating, vomiting, and breathing difficulties follow a deadly scorpion's sting. The victim might foam at the mouth or be blinded. Death can occur very quickly.

Scorpions like to sleep in warm, dark places. The danger for humans comes when they crawl into bedding or shoes or sneak underneath carpets. A scorpion will lash out with its tail when a barefoot person steps on it. In scorpion country, always shake out your shoes before putting them on in the morning.

MILLIPEDE
27 years

C ould you walk if you had eight legs? How about eighty? How about two hundred? How would you coordinate all those legs so you could move forward without tripping over a dozen or so of your own appendages?

The millipede is a remarkable animal simply because of all its legs. The word *millipede* actually means "thousand-footed," but no millipede has a thousand feet. There are about 12,351 species of millipedes worldwide, some with as few as twenty legs, some with hundreds more. The record holder not only has the most legs of any animal in the world, it also has a remarkable life span.

First discovered in 1926, *Illacme plenipes* was found living in a tiny patch of ground in San Benito County, California. It was rediscovered (after being lost?) almost eighty years later, in November 2005. When scientists began to study this creature, they found that females had as many as 750 legs (males only had a maximum of 402). It was further discovered that females continued to add body segments as they grew. And these particular arthropods lived to be 27 years old.

Most millipedes are very clumsy and slow. Their legs are designed for moving through loose soil and humus rather than scurrying out in the open. There are, however, a few predatory species that can move very rapidly when attacking their prey.

Because centipedes also have lots of legs, many people confuse them with millipedes. Centipedes (often referred to as "hundred-leggers") have one pair of legs per body segment (the genus *Geophilus* has the most legs: 177 pairs) and typically move in an S-shaped pattern. Millipedes, with two pairs of legs on each body segment, move in a straight line without wiggling. Centipedes also have longer legs than millipedes, with the legs in the back longer than those in the front. The legs of millipedes are all the same size. Even though millipedes have more legs than centipedes, they walk much slower.

When disturbed, millipedes coil up into a tight ball so their enemies cannot get at them. The largest millipede in the world is the giant African millipede *(Archispirostreptus gigas)*. At least one of these monsters has been measured at 15.2 inches long.

Several varieties of tropical millipedes give off a foul-smelling odor when disturbed. They do this through a series of glands located along both sides of their bodies. Some species can spray the fluid produced by these glands a distance of more than 2 feet. The fluid contains cyanide, which temporarily blinds or injures any enemy looking to make the millipede a meal. The millipede then has time to escape into the soil or nearby vegetation.

QUEEN ANT
28 years

I have a particular fondness for ants. Maybe it's their social nature that impresses me the most. You see, each ant has a crop and a stomach. The stomach digests the food, and the crop is used to store it for regurgitative feeding. After an ant has finished eating for itself, it's always willing to share the contents of its crop with a companion, associate, or even a casual date. In my book, that's not only economical, it's sharing of the highest order.

Ants have lived on earth for more than one hundred million years. While many other animals (think dinosaurs) have died out, ants have thrived. Today, they are among the most widespread of all insects. Biologists have calculated that the combined weight of all the ants on the planet is equal to the combined weight of all the people. There are 8,000 to 9,500 species of ants throughout the world, with 700 species in North America. These range from microscopic species to a few well over an inch long.

The one creature that does more for its particular species is the queen ant. Imagine spending your entire adult life lying around the house doing nothing but birthing thousands of offspring every year. That's the "job" of the queen. In fact, an entire ant colony revolves around its queen. With rare exceptions, she is the only one in the colony that lays eggs—all of an ant colony's members are her offspring.

When an ant colony begins to grow too large, winged male and female ants leave it, mate while flying, then search for a new nesting site. Once a suitable site is located, they shed their wings, and the males die. When the nest has been established, the new queen digs a burrow and closes herself in. And she begins to lay eggs . . . thousands and thousands of eggs. Depending on the species, a queen may lay up to thirty thousand eggs *every day*. Over the course of her 28-year life, she may produce more than thirty-two million offspring.

MARINE IGUANA

29 years

W hen you want to eat, you go to a grocery store, a fast food restaurant, or your refrigerator. You're able to eat many different kinds of food and can find that food in many different places. Unlike you, the marine iguana eats only one type of food—and it must dive underwater to find it.

The marine iguana is a remarkable creature simply because it can be found entirely on one group of islands, the famed Galapagos Islands, located 600 miles off the western coast of Ecuador. Home to some of the most unusual plant and animal species in the world, the chain inspired Charles Darwin to write *On the Origin of Species by Means of Natural Selection or the Preservation of Favored Races in the Struggle for Life* (Darwin was not, apparently, noted for his brevity).

One Galapagos species, the marine iguana, feeds entirely on the algae that grow on underwater rocks. Because it has partially webbed feet, this iguana can easily swim beneath the waves. It has strong claws that help it hold on to the slippery rocks as it feeds. Occasionally, iguanas will swim out beyond the surf to feed, where their chief enemy, the shark, may catch an unsuspecting diner or two.

When they dive, marine iguanas can go 35 feet below the surface. Mostly, though, they dine on algae-covered rocks 15 to 20 feet deep. Although they can stay underwater up to an hour, most iguanas remain submerged for only about 5 to 10 minutes while feeding. The marine iguana is the only lizard that uses the sea as its sole source of food.

When they're not eating, marine iguanas gather together in tight bunches on the rocky shore, often piling on top of one another. Here they bask in the sun, raising their body temperatures, then return to the water in search of more food. As they sun themselves, finches and mockingbirds crawl over them, helpfully removing blood-sucking ticks from the iguana's skin (the ticks are an important part of the birds' diet).

The life span of lizards depends on the species. Most scientists agree that the larger the species, the longer it is likely to live. One of the rarest lizards in the world, the komodo dragon of Indonesia, grows to more than 8 feet long, reaches a weight of 200 pounds, and lives for about 20 years. There is at least one unsubstantiated report of a captive Mexican beaded lizard (up to 36 inches in length and weighing more than 6 pounds) living for nearly 34 years. It is suspected that the peaceful existence of marine iguanas in the Galapagos may be a contributing factor in their relatively long lizard life spans of up to 29 years.

Although a marine iguana looks fearsome, it is a very mild-mannered creature. Occasionally, males will engage in territorial fights in which they butt their heads together or push each other around with their heads (behavior somewhat similar to what you might see at a tailgate party). When startled, a marine iguana will blow saltwater vapor from glands in its nose, making it look like a miniature dragon.

VAMPIRE BAT

29 + years

eople in 18th-century Europe had many superstitions about creatures of the night. Lack of scientific knowledge, along with vivid imaginations, contributed to the belief that all nocturnal animals were dangerous. Since these creatures were rarely seen, descriptions of their habits and size were often greatly exaggerated. Some of the most-told stories of this time centered on one particular being—the vampire—that attacked unsuspecting people in the dark. Assuming the form of a bat (since bats were well-known nocturnal creatures), this beast sucked the blood of defenseless humans while they slept. Tales of the bloodsucker, along with the popularity of Bram Stoker's 1897 book *Dracula* (and all the subsequent movie versions), perpetuated the belief that all bats were blood-sucking animals. Not true at all.

Although there are about 1,100 species of bats worldwide, there are only 3 separate species of vampire bats: the common vampire bat, white-winged vampire bat, and hairy-legged vampire bat.

Vampire bats live in the tropical and subtropical regions of North and South America, ranging from northern Mexico to central Chile and Argentina. They grow to lengths of 2 or 3 inches and weigh about 1 to 2 ounces. They are among the world's smallest bats.

During the day, vampire bats hang upside down in caves or old mines in colonies of up to two thousand individuals. At night, they leave their roosts and search out victims. They usually attack domesticated animals—horses, cows, mules, pigs, chickens, and goats—but will also attack small wild animals. (Yes, they've been known to attack humans, too, but this occurs very rarely.)

In reality, vampire bats are technically not bloodsuckers— they are actually blood-lappers. They usually attack while their prey is asleep. They use heat sensors located just above their noses to select a spot on the victim, usually on the foot or leg, where blood vessels lie close to the surface. The bat softens the skin by licking it, then makes a quick bite with its razor-sharp incisors. These specialized teeth make a shallow wound by slashing away a small piece of the victim's skin. The incision is done so precisely that the victim often doesn't wake up. Using its muscular, grooved tongue, the bat laps up blood that flows from the wound. Usually a vampire bat drinks about an ounce of blood from a victim. Sometimes, however, it laps up so much blood that it's unable to fly away. Then it has to wait several hours until the meal is digested before it can return to its roost. Like Dracula, the vampire bat's entire diet consists of blood—it eats no solid food.

As the bat feeds, substances in its saliva prevent blood from coagulating. Scientists have discovered that the vampire bat's anticoagulant is twenty-five times more effective than any manufactured anticoagulant.

Bats in the wild usually live between 12 and 15 years. However, if a vampire bat is raised in a cushy university laboratory, it can expect a much longer life. In one case, a captive vampire bat lived for 29.2 years before it went off to the great blood bank in the sky.

PENGUIN

29 + years

If you want to live an uncomplicated life, you probably don't want to be a penguin. Penguin lives are anything but easy, and elderly penguins are more of an anomaly than one would think from watching Disney movies. One of the oldest penguins on record, a southern rockhopper named Rocky who lived at the Bergen Aquarium in Norway, lasted for 29 years and 4 months, greatly exceeding the average 15- to 20-year penguin life span.

There are between 17 and 20 species of penguins in the world, all of which live in the southern hemisphere. While we often associate penguins with Antarctica, they are not always found in cold climates. Several species live in temperate zones, and one, the Galapagos penguin, lives near the equator.

Almost every species of penguin suffers a high mortality rate. Researchers estimate that at least 50 percent of king penguin chicks die as a result of winter starvation, and up to 90 percent of emperor chicks die within their first year. Penguins face a near-constant threat from all manner of predators on both land and water. They are hunted by foxes, snakes, dogs, cats, leopard and fur seals, sea lions, sharks, and killer whales.

Other birds are also a persistent enemy. These winged predators feast on chicks that wander from nests or are too weak to defend themselves. Skuas, ibises, and gulls attack egg-filled nests, sometimes destroying up to 40 percent of the unhatched population. Birds known as sheathbills sometimes stand next to baby chinstrap penguins and intercept the regurgitated food from the parents as adult penguins attempt to feed their young.

Penguin populations are affected by humans, too. For centuries, indigenous people have taken penguin eggs and penguins themselves for food. Penguins were an easy prey because of their inability to fly as well as a basic lack of fear. Penguin feathers, skins, oil, guano, and meat have all been lucrative commercial ventures for generations of coastal inhabitants around the world.

There is now evidence that the activity of cruise ships (sometimes operating in the name of ecotourism) in Antarctic waters might also have a negative impact on indigenous penguins. Then there's the weather: A 1982 study blamed El Niño for a 65 percent depletion of the Humboldt penguin population off the coast of Peru. Suffice it to say that penguins as a whole are threatened on many different fronts.

Although penguins lead difficult lives, they have endured. Scientists in New Zealand uncovered what are believed to be the world's oldest penguin fossils. These 58- to 60-million-year-old bones belong to four specimens from an ancient genus of penguin known as Waimanu. One researcher, after an analysis of Waimanu DNA, postulates that these fossils make a "strong case" for modern birds appearing shortly after the dinosaurs died out, some 65 million years ago.

DOG

29 + years

Ever since the gray wolf was domesticated, about fifteen thousand years ago, dogs have become one of the most ubiquitous animals on the planet. For centuries, dogs have been bred for a range of tasks, including pulling wagons, herding sheep, tracking prey, guarding valuables, and warning their owners of danger. Modern dog breeds demonstrate more variation in size, appearance, and behavior than almost any other species.

The typical life spans of dogs vary according to adult size, which is often determined by breed. On average, smaller dogs live to be about 15 to 16. Medium and large dogs usually live for 10 to 13 years, and very large breeds such as mastiffs will often live for 7 or 8. The following lists several popular breeds and their average life expectancies:

Bulldog: 6 years
Irish wolfhound: 6 years
Great dane: 8 years
Doberman pinscher: 9 years
Boxer: 10 years
Irish setter: 11 years
Cocker spaniel: 12 years
Standard poodle: 12 years
Chihuahua: 13 years
Dachshund: 14 years

The long-standing myth that 1 "human year" is equivalent to 7 "dog years" is not true. As a rough approximation, the human equivalent of a 1-year-old dog is between about 10 and 15 years. A 1-year-old dog for most breeds has generally reached its full growth and is sexually mature. The second year is equivalent to another 3 to 8 human years in terms of physical and mental maturity, and each year thereafter is equivalent to about 4 or 5. According to researchers at the University of California, Davis, small-breed dogs become geriatric at about 11, medium breeds at 10, large breeds at 8, and giant breeds at 7.

Some notable dogs have lived far longer than these ranges, however.

- Bluey was a cattle dog who worked in Australia for nearly 20 years before retiring. He died in 1939, at the age of 29 years, 5 months. (Another Australian dog, a cattle dog-labrador mix, died in 1984, reportedly at the age of 32 years, 3 days, but this case has not been fully documented.)
- Bella, a Labrador cross, had reached the ripe old age of 29 when she suffered a heart attack and died, in 2008, according to her owner, David Richardson in England. She is currently the world record holder.
- Before Bella, the record for the oldest dog was held by Butch, a 28-year-old from Virginia who died in 2003.

Suffice it to say there will always be much disagreement (and perhaps a little fudging) when discussing the longevity of dogs. Dog lovers, like cat lovers, tend to exaggerate the ages of their pets. It seems the more we love our critters, the more we want to extol their virtues, which is why there will probably never be an argument about the longest-living house fly.

SNAIL

30 years

Most animals have two, four, or eight feet, and they come in pairs. Snails, however, are part of a group called gastropods, or "belly-foots," that travel around on their stomachs, which are actually their feet.

When a snail "walks," it moves forward by generating a series of waves along the length of its foot. These waves pass from the front to the back of the foot, creating a rippling motion.

As it moves, the snail excretes a slimy substance from just behind its head. This slime helps it safely travel over rough surfaces and sharp objects—a snail can climb over a razor blade without cutting itself. The slime track is not a continuous smear; it's actually a series of patches where the snail's foot has come into contact with the ground.

Snails live in damp places among plants, under stones, and in the soil. They are most active when the weather is wet. When it's dry, snails are frequently inactive, attaching themselves to a wall or tree trunk and withdrawing into their shells. This brief period of inactivity is called estivation. It's similar to hibernation, when snails bury themselves under several inches of soil, slow their bodily functions, and remain inactive over the winter. In very dry areas or cold regions, snails can hibernate for up to 4 years.

The life span of snails varies from species to species. In the wild, *Achatinidae* snails live around 5 to 7 years, and most *Helix* snails live about 2 to 3. Aquatic apple snails live only a year or so. Most snail deaths are due to predators or parasites. In captivity, the life span of snails is much longer, ranging from 10 to 15 years. The roman snail, a well-known and often-eaten species in Europe (it's also known as escargot), has been known to live for up to 30 years.

Snails can be found all over the world but are primarily concentrated in areas where there is lots of vegetation, moisture, and warm weather. Some of the largest snails are found in Africa. One specimen of the giant African land snail collected in Sierra Leone in 1976 weighed 2 pounds and measured over 15 inches from snout to tail. These enormous snails spend much of their time eating various plants and fruits, such as bananas. They have also been discovered eating dead animals. All snails, no matter what their size, have up to twenty thousand teeth . . . on their tongues.

A snail also has two sets of tentacles. The longer, upper pair have eyes at the tips that can distinguish between light and dark. The other set is much shorter and used to feel objects as the snail moves. They are also used to sense sound by detecting vibrations. Both sets of tentacles can be pulled into the snail's head at will.

RATTLESNAKE

30 years

Rattlesnakes belong to a group of snakes known as pit vipers. These snakes have small depressions, or pits, on both sides of their faces, between the eyes and the nostrils. These pits are used as temperature detectors, primarily to locate prey in the dark. They are so sensitive that from 6 feet away, a rattlesnake can detect a 0.009-degree rise in temperature caused by an approaching animal. One study showed that a rattlesnake could detect the heat from a candle flame 30 feet away.

Most folks would agree that the most distinctive feature of the rattlesnake is its rattle. This unique structure is made of six to fourteen dry, interlocking rings of skin. When a rattlesnake is alarmed, it vibrates its tail, and the thickened pieces of skin rub against one another to create a hair-raising buzz. There really isn't anything inside the rattle. The segments simply clatter against each other to make the sound. An agitated snake can move its rattle back and forth at a rate of approximately 60 or more times per second. It's a very loud and very clear signal to stay away.

Many people believe the number of rattles can determine a rattlesnake's age. This isn't true. Each time a rattlesnake sheds its skin, a new segment is added to the rattle, but shedding is not an annual event. When it occurs is determined by a number of factors, including temperature and the snake's diet. As a result, it is impossible to determine a rattlesnake's age by its rattle. It has been documented, however, that rattlesnakes can live up to 30 years in captivity.

The diet of a rattlesnake consists primarily of small, warm-blooded animals, such as rodents and rabbits. They also occasionally feed on frogs, salamanders, and lizards. Rattlesnakes attack larger animals, such as cattle or humans, only when they are disturbed.

Rattlesnakes produce venom, modified saliva used primarily for hunting, in a gland behind their eyes. The gland is surrounded by a series of muscles that contract and force venom down tubelike ducts to the base of the fangs. When a rattlesnake bites, its fangs enter and leave the victim in less than a second. The venom is injected into the prey through both fangs. Fangs are replaced every few weeks. They wear out quickly, so up to six replacements are continually growing in each jaw. When not in use, a rattlesnake's fangs are "folded" inside its mouth.

Because of their sharp, pointy teeth, rattlesnakes cannot chew their prey. Instead, their venom acts like stomach juices. It not only kills the victim, it also aids in digestion. After prey is killed, the injected venom breaks down the animal's insides. In a few minutes, the victim gets soft and squishy, and the rattlesnake swallows it whole.

TYRANNOSAURUS REX

30 years

hen most people think of dinosaurs, they think of *Tyrannosaurus rex*, perhaps the most famous of all prehistoric creatures. *T. rex* was certainly the biggest and heaviest carnivorous dinosaur, reaching a length of 40 feet, a height of 18 feet, and a body weight of nearly 7 tons. Research has also revealed that *T. rex*'s brain was about the size of a sweet potato, which just goes to show that you don't have to be smart to be popular.

Tyrannosaurus rex lived about 65 million years ago in what is now Montana, Wyoming, and South Dakota, as well as the Canadian province of Alberta. During this time, the north-central part of the United States was a lush environment of forests and streams, an ideal location for plant-eaters and the carnivores that fed on them.

Determining the life span of *T. rex* (or any dinosaur, for that matter) is a lot like predicting who will win the lottery. There's a lot of guessing, conjecture, and speculation. Nevertheless, paleontologists in Canada may have found part of the answer. By examining the metatarsals, or foot bones, of twenty-two *Albertosauruses*, a relative of *Tyrannosaurus*, excavated from a single site in Alberta (one of the world's largest sources of dinosaur remains), they were able to determine that the life span of these dinosaurs was about 30 years. (In comparison, some modern-day reptiles can live 50 to 100 years, or longer.)

The researchers found that mortality rates for *Albertosaurus* were high in the first 2 years of life, possibly due to infant predation, then sharply lower until the teenage years. After age 13, the rates jumped to 23 percent. One of the paleontologists speculates that combat during prime mating years is a possible reason why the mortality rate spiked.

Scientists at the Field Museum in Chicago have been studying the bones of Sue, the resident *Tyrannosaurus rex* (and the museum's most popular exhibit since it was unveiled in 2000). They have been able to determine *T. rex*'s growth pattern and life span using an innovative technique that could be applied to other dinosaurs. They determined Sue's age by counting growth lines in her bones then calculating the body size from circumference measurements of the femur. Correlating these two sets of data resulted in a distinctive growth curve.

The research determined that Sue was 28 when she died and that she reached her full size (14,000 pounds) 9 years before her death. During a teenage growth spurt, she gained up to 4.6 pounds per day. These numbers were instrumental in estimating an average *T. rex* life span of about 30 years, a third of which would have been spent as an adult.

The research also showed that a *Tyrannosaurus rex*'s life was not easy. Sue's ribs indicated that several had been broken during her life, and her fibula has a lump that might have been caused by a nasty infection.

Her life may have also been affected by another deadly factor. Scientists in South Dakota have unearthed three *Tyrannosaurus* skeletons that indicate that *T. rex* was cannibalistic. One of the skulls had a hole in the back matching the shape of a *T. rex* tooth. Another skeleton had a 6-inch-long *T. rex* tooth embedded in a broken rib. Fatal wounds on the left side of its skull were the result of another *T. rex* bite. A third specimen had vertebrae that had been bitten in half, along with several bones that had been chewed out of the skeleton. *Tyrannosaurus rex* seems to have lived up to the meaning of its name: tyrant lizard.

It is known that these creatures engaged in ferocious battles in defense of their territories. Research is still being conducted to determine why *T. rexs* might have feasted on one another. Some scientists speculate that it may have been because there were few, if any, other animals to attack. It's likely, then, that *T. rex* could have turned on a member of its own group just to get a quick meal.

TARANTULA

30 years

The tarantula is one scary-looking animal. Hairy legs and fangs that are longer than those of many venomous snakes make this spider one of the most feared in the world. In reality, however, the tarantula looks more dangerous than it is. To date, there have been no known reports of human fatalities from tarantula bites—just severe pain and temporary numbness.

The largest tarantula in the world is the vividly named goliath bird-eating spider *(Theraphosa blondi)* of South America. This giant weighs up to 4 ounces and has a 12-inch leg span, larger than an average dinner plate. The female has an abdomen about the size of a tennis ball. The species sports fangs that can be nearly ¾ inch long. One of the smallest known tarantulas, *Aphonopelma paloma*, found in Arizona, has a total adult body length of ⅓ inch—its entire body is shorter than the fangs of the goliath. True to its name, the goliath bird-eating spider dines on baby birds, as well as bats, rats, frogs, insects, small snakes, and lizards.

Research indicates that tarantulas live from 25 to 30 years in captivity. The common North American species *Eurypelma californicum* has a recorded life span of 30 years, with females significantly outliving males. The oldest known tarantula ancestor is *Rosamygale grauvogeli*, found in France in a fossil from the Lower Triassic Period (235 to 240 million years ago).

There are approximately 920 different species of tarantulas distributed throughout the world, primarily in tropical and subtropical countries. Most of the tarantulas sold in North American pet stores have been imported from other countries, principally Mexico. About 30 species are native to the United States.

Tarantulas dig and live in small burrows, where they patiently wait for prey. Their primary food is small invertebrates: flies, crickets, grasshoppers, and beetles. When a tarantula locates a victim, it pounces and sinks its fangs deep into the victim's body. In order to gain leverage, it often lifts its body. The downward thrust of the fangs pins the victim so venom can easily be injected.

When it dies, the victim is carried to the tarantula's den to be devoured. Tarantulas don't have teeth for tearing and chewing. Instead, they regurgitate powerful digestive juices onto their victims. Tarantulas slurp nutrients from predigested prey with their sucking stomachs. After a meal, they leave behind a hollow carcass.

The tarantula's greatest enemy is the tarantula hawk, a large wasp. This insect attacks by injecting venom that paralyzes the spider but does not kill it. The wasp drags the spider to its burrow and lays an egg inside its body. When the baby wasp hatches, it eats the spider alive from the inside.

GIRAFFE

33 years

A giraffe's neck is one of the longest, in proportion to overall body length, in the animal kingdom. As expected, these creatures often engage in some serious necking. For giraffes, however, necking usually means a fight. During combat, which typically occurs between two males, giraffes often throw their necks and heads at each other in an effort to knock their opponent to the ground.

When Europeans first saw the giraffe, in the fifteenth century, they were certain that the animal was a biological anomaly. The ancestors of modern giraffes most likely evolved in south-central Europe about eight million years ago. The exact number of giraffe species in the world is disputed. Some experts contend that there are two species (*Giraffa reticulate* and *Giraffa camelopardalis*) with ten subspecies. Some believe there is only a single species (*G. camelopardalis*) with either five, six, eight, or nine subspecies, depending on who you ask.

After a gestation period of 14 to 15 months, a female giraffe gives birth, and she does this standing up, dropping the infant about 5 feet straight to the ground. Young giraffes are exceeding vulnerable—prime targets for lions, hyenas, leopards, and wild dogs. As a result, the mother will stay with a newborn almost all the time. Even so, as few as 25 percent of newborn giraffes reach adulthood.

Giraffes have been popular zoo attractions since the first one was brought to Paris in the early 1800s. In the wild, a giraffe can expect a life of about 20 to 25 years. They live longer in captivity. One giraffe, Hildy, a lifelong resident of the Dallas Zoo, was born on October 9, 1973, and passed away on September 11, 2007, at age 33. She is believed to be the oldest giraffe on record.

Some fascinating giraffe facts:

- A giraffe has the same number of neck vertebrae (seven) as you do.
- Each giraffe has a unique pattern of spots.
- Both male and female giraffes have horns.
- A giraffe's front legs are 10 percent longer than its back legs.
- An adult giraffe's heart weighs approximately 22 pounds (the average weight of a human heart is 8 to 12 ounces).

STARFISH

35 years

Found in all the world's oceans, starfish—more appropriately called sea stars, since they are not fish at all—are some of nature's most incredible creatures. There are approximately 1,800 species of starfish, with some of the most unusual found in tropical waters. Starfish can have as few as four arms or as many as forty. At the end of each arm is a small eye able to sense light and dark. Depending on the species, starfish can range in size from 0.4 inch *(Patiriella parvivipara)* to 3 feet in diameter *(Pycnopodia helianthoides)*, which is about the size of a flattened beach ball. No matter what their size, the creatures have no brains or blood.

Female starfish produce up to sixty-five million eggs in a typical spawning season. Juvenile mortality is extremely high; the eggs are consumed by a variety of marine organisms. Most species of starfish can live for about 3 to 5 years, but few actually reach that age. Some species can reach age 35 and a weight of 11 pounds.

Starfish move using tube feet on the undersides of their arms. These "feet" are actually hollow muscular cylinders filled with water. When starfish walk, the feet are pushed out hydraulically by the contraction of muscular sacs. At the tips of the feet are suction discs that help starfish stick to rocks. Starfish walk by affixing their suckers to the rocks and pulling themselves forward. In several species, one of the starfish's arms nearly always takes the lead when the starfish is walking; in other species, it is more usual for the arms to take turns leading the way. The typical speed for a starfish is about 2 to 3 inches a minute.

One amazing feature of the starfish is its ability to regenerate lost arms. This process can take up to an entire year to complete. Some starfish can regenerate from a remnant of arm no more than ½ inch long. *Linckia* starfish can actually pull in opposite directions until they break into two parts. Each part can then grow into a new animal.

Starfish have a good sense of smell, which helps them locate prey and avoid predators. Even though they have no teeth, they are carnivorous. Typically, they feed on clams, mollusks, worms, crustaceans, oysters, fish, and carrion. They eat shellfish by positioning themselves over the shell of their intended victim, gripping a nearby rock with one arm, or a few, and holding both halves of an oyster or clamshell with others. Then they begin to pull the two halves apart. A starfish may need to pull for several hours or even several days before it separates the shell. Once a small gap has been opened, the starfish inserts the lobes of its stomach inside to digest the bivalve. Starfish are one of the few animals that can push their stomachs out of their bodies and turn them inside out to eat a meal. They don't make great dinner guests.

In some parts of the world, starfish are a major ecological problem. They eat coral and can be found in great numbers along many of the world's coral reefs, including the Great Barrier Reef of Australia. Here, starfish are destroying large sections of the reef, which has been built up over thousands of years.

TRICERATOPS

35 years (?)

Look at any child's collection of dinosaur toys and you're sure to find *Triceratops*. This Late Cretaceous (sixty-eight to sixty-five million years ago) beast lived throughout what is now North America. Fossils have been discovered as far north as Saskatchewan and Alberta and as far south as Colorado. An individual *Triceratops* reached a weight of 6 to 12 tons, a length of 26 to 29 feet from front to back, and a height of 9 to 10 feet. The beast would be equivalent to two modern-day black rhinoceroses packed into a single creature.

The *Triceratops'* most distinctive feature was its skull, which could reach almost a third of the length of the entire animal (by comparison, our skull is about an eighth of our height). Recent studies of the skull case have indicated that *Triceratops'* brain was about the same size as a closed human fist.

At the back of the *Triceratops'* skull was an impressive, bony frill, which could often extend to nearly 7 feet in length. There is much disagreement about its function. Some paleontologists believe the frill helped protect the dinosaur's vulnerable neck area from would-be predators. Unfortunately, this contention is undercut by discoveries of *Tyrannosaurus rex* bite marks on frill remains, suggesting that the frill may not have been a very successful deterrent.

Some scientists postulate that the frill helped *Triceratops* regulate its body temperature. Still others believe that it may have been used in mating displays or to help *Triceratops* identify members of its own species. Since there are no living

Triceratops around to ask, I suppose paleontologists will just have to keep speculating.

There has also been considerable disagreement among scientists as to the function of the dinosaur's three horns. Early thinking was that they were used for defensive purposes. However, many scientists now believe the horns were likely used in courtship and dominance displays—similar to the way in which reindeer and other ungulates use their antlers. Despite cartoons, children's books, and movies illustrating *Triceratops* in mortal combat with its supposed archenemy *Tyrannosaurus rex*, there is little evidence that *Triceratops* used its horns as primary weapons.

In spite of its fearsome appearance, this prehistoric tank was an herbivore. It browsed primarily on a range of low-growing plants that might have included ferns, cycads, and grasses. Given its enormous size, it is likely that *Triceratops* required great quantities of plant material each day in order to maintain its bulk. Its jaws ended in a deep, narrow beak that may have been used to pluck fibrous plants. What is less known is that *Triceratops* had between 432 and 800 teeth in its mouth, all arranged in batteries and stacked in rows three to five high. Like modern-day sharks that continually shed and replace their teeth, tooth replacement for *Triceratops* was continuous.

What we don't know for certain was the average life span of this creature. There is a great deal of speculation based on its average size and weight (larger dinosaurs tended to live longer than smaller ones) as well as on its metabolic rate. Its life span may well have ranged anywhere from that of a *Tyrannosaurus rex* (30 years) all the way up to that of a *Diplodocus* (100 years). Using some known information about other dinosaur ages, we might employ a simple extrapolation to calculate the estimated maximum age of *Triceratops*.

Here's what we know about some selected dinosaurs:

Tyrannosaurus rex
    average weight: 14,000 pounds
    estimated maximum age: 30 years
Diplodocus
    average weight: 40,000 pounds
    estimated maximum age: 100 years
Bothriospondylus madagascariensis
    average weight: 38,500 pounds
    estimated maximum age: 43 years

With this information, we might speculate (and it is, most certainly, pure speculation) that *Triceratops* had a maximum life span of approximately 35 years. There's no way to be certain, of course, and it remains to be confirmed. For now, we can look at it this way: *Triceratops* probably lived longer than your average sea cucumber, but not as long as a quahog clam.

CAT

38 years

I t has often been said that there are only two types of people in the world: those who love, adore, admire, idolize, appreciate, and worship cats—and those who don't. It is estimated that there are between sixty and ninety million cats in the United States, so it seems reasonable to assume that the number of people in that first category is considerable. Since there are just over three hundred million people in this country, that means that there is about one cat for every four people.

According to veterinarians, the average life expectancy of a cat is often dependent on its sex. Male cats live, on average, from 13 to 15 years. Females, on the other hand, average between 15 and 17 years. Life expectancy is also dependent on whether a cat is primarily an indoor cat or outdoor cat. In general, indoor cats will live from 12 to 18 years, with many living into their 20s. Since there is no evidence to the contrary, this writer believes that the extended life of an indoor cat is due primarily to a fluffy pillow in the master bedroom and a ceramic bowl in the kitchen regularly supplied with fish-flavored treats.

Outdoor cats tend to have considerably shorter lives, often averaging 4 to 5 years. Their relatively brief life spans are due to any number of factors, including dog attacks, car accidents, and deadly viruses spread by contact with infected animals.

Most vets will tell you that a cat who reaches age 10 is considered a senior citizen. If that's the case, then Creme Puff, a cat owned by Jake Perry of Austin, Texas, is the most senior of senior citizens, at least in the cat world. Recognized by the *Guinness*

Book of World Records as the world's oldest authenticated cat, Creme Puff, born on August 3, 1967, died on August 6, 2005, reaching the grand old age of 38 years, 3 days. It would be safe to say that this feline was an indoor cat who was loved, adored, admired, and idolized throughout its nearly four-decade life.

Some fascinating feline facts:

- Cats have three eyelids.
- Cats purr at 26 cycles per second.
- In ancient Egypt, when a cat died, the whole family shaved their eyebrows in mourning.
- Cats have about forty more bones than humans do.
- The night vision of cats is about six times better than a human's.
- Cats spend about 30 percent of their waking hours grooming.
- There are thirty-three recognized breeds of cats.
- According to the American Pet Products Manufacturers Association, 13 percent of cat owners buy birthday presents for their pets.
- Benjamin Franklin, Abraham Lincoln, George Washington, and Mark Twain all loved cats.
- Julius Caesar, William Shakespeare, Napoleon Bonaparte, and Dwight D. Eisenhower were all noted felinophobes.

SLOTH

40 years

One of the most unusual animals in the world, the sloth spends almost its entire life upside down. It not only walks upside down through the trees, it also mates, gives birth to its babies, and sleeps while it hangs upside down. In fact, sloths may sleep for more than twenty-four hours hanging from the branches of a tree.

There are six different species of sloths divided into two groups: the two-toed sloths (two species) and three-toed sloths (four species). Two-toed sloths can be found from Honduras to Northern Argentina; three-toed sloths can be found from Venezuela to Brazil. The two-toed sloth is more common than the three-toed and is the type most often seen in zoos. Both types actually have three toes on their hind limbs; the two-toed sloth has two toes or "fingers" on its forelimbs instead of three. The average life span of a two-toed sloth is about 20 years in the wild. However, ages of 40 years have been recorded for sloths in captivity.

A sloth "walks" very unhurriedly through a tree and is one of the slowest-moving animals in the world. The average speed for a sloth is about 4 feet a minute. The fastest recorded speed for a three-toed sloth is 0.068 mph, which works out to 6 feet per minute.

Sloths belong to the order of animals known as Xenarthra, which means "strange joints." The name refers to the creature's vertebral joints, which have extra articulations and are unlike those of any other mammal. They serve to strengthen the lower back and hips, providing extra strength to the forelegs in activities not associated with locomotion, such as digging and hanging from branches.

Sloths hang from trees by means of long, curved claws that look like meat hooks. Their arms are considerably longer than their legs and are ideally suited for an upside-down life. Amazingly, sloths cannot walk upright on their arms and legs. Whenever they are on the ground they must slowly drag themselves along. About once a week, they slowly crawl down from the trees to urinate and defecate, which they do in communal areas. Why sloths do not eliminate their wastes from up in the trees is one of the great unanswered questions of science.

Another distinguishing feature of sloths is their hair, which grows from their bellies to their backs (in most mammals, hair grows from the top of the back to the stomach). Because sloths live upside down in a very wet environment, their "opposite growing" hair allows rainwater to run off. Sloth hair is usually covered by a layer of green algae that helps conceal the animal from enemies. Their green color and sluggish habits make sloths look like masses of leaves lodged in the treetops.

Sloths feed entirely on the vegetation they find in the trees of Central and South American rain forests. This diet has high cellulose content and so sloths have very complex stomachs and a lengthy digestive process. Meals may take up to a month to digest. It's been estimated by some biologists that a third of a sloth's weight might be made up solely of its stomach contents.

MUTE SWAN

40 years

One of the most recognizable creatures to ever grace a river, pond, or lake, the mute swan is native to most of western and central Europe. A migratory bird, it can also be found throughout the northern latitudes and as far south as North Africa and the Mediterranean. Introduced into the United States in the late 1800s, mute swans can be found along the eastern seaboard and across the Great Lakes. Worldwide, their population numbers are estimated to be in the hundreds of thousands. Mute swan fossils estimated to be 6,000 years old have been discovered in Great Britain, while 10,000-year-old fossils of mute swan ancestors have been located in Idaho, Oregon, Arizona, and California.

Mute swans are some of the largest of all waterfowl. Adults can stand over 4 feet tall and have a body length that ranges from 49 to 67 inches and a wingspan of almost 9 feet. Males average about 27 pounds and females weigh in at around 19 pounds. Despite their name, mute swans are not silent, but their calls are very quiet and do not carry very far. They make a snorting *heorrr* and will hiss when agitated.

Unlike most animals, the mute swan is reported to mate for life. Changing of mates does occur, but usually only when a partner dies. If a male loses its mate and pairs with a young female, she joins him on his territory. If he mates with an older female, they go to hers. If a female loses its mate, she re-mates quickly and usually chooses a younger male (not unlike some famous Hollywood stars).

The mute swan has become a symbol of beauty, grace, tranquility, love, and a host of other anthropomorphic expressions. Its image can be found on hotel marquees, soap bar wrappings, postcards, beauty aids, tissues, and snack foods, to name a few. It has been celebrated in story ("The Ugly Duckling") and pictured on money (the euro), and it's the national bird of Denmark.

The life expectancy of mute swans in the wild may reach 25 years; the average, however, is probably closer to 7. The oldest documented mute swan was found on Christmas Day 2008 in Denmark. It was dead but had been tagged—a small numbered metal ring was fastened around its leg. When the ring was sent to the Copenhagen Bird Ringing Centre at the Zoological Museum at the University of Copenhagen, an examination revealed that the swan had been tagged on February 21, 1970, in northern Germany, when it was $1^{1}/_{2}$ years old—making it at least 40 when it died.

POLAR BEAR

43 + years

Known as the world's largest land carnivore, the polar bear is native to arctic regions and can be found in only five countries: Denmark (Greenland), Norway, Russia, Canada, and the United States (in Alaska). It is estimated that there are between twenty thousand and twenty-five thousand polar bears worldwide, although they are suffering steep declines in population. The International Union for Conservation of Nature now lists global warming as the most significant threat to the polar bear, primarily because the melting of its sea ice habitat reduces the bear's ability to find food. The IUCN states, "If climatic trends continue, polar bears may become extirpated from most of their range within 100 years."

In the wild, polar bears typically live for 10 to 18 years. It's quite rare for a wild polar bear to live into its 20s, although it's not unusual for captive individuals to reach age 30 or older. Extended life spans for captive individuals may be due to a combination of factors, including genetic inheritance, special care by zookeepers, a balanced diet, and plenty of exercise (except for the zookeepers, these are the same factors that contribute to long life in humans).

The current longevity record for a polar bear is 43 years, 8 months, held by Doris, a wild-born female who lived most of her life at the Detroit Zoo. She died in 1991. In second place is Debbie, who, until her death in November 2008, lived at the Assiniboine Park Zoo in Winnipeg, Canada. Over the last few months of her life, Debbie suffered a series of strokes, was losing weight rapidly, and had blood in her urine. When she suffered multiple organ failure, it was decided that she should be euthanized. After she was put down, it was determined that she had reached the age of 42. At the time of her death, Debbie had been seen by more than 18 million zoo visitors, making her the most popular attraction in the zoo's 100-plus-year history.

Most old polar bears in the wild die from starvation or exposure—they become too weak to catch food and eventually succumb to the elements. Bears injured in fights or accidents might either die from their injuries or become unable to hunt effectively, leading to starvation. Unfortunately, the exact causes of wild polar bear deaths are not well understood since carcasses are rarely found.

COW

48 years

The next time you pour yourself a glass of milk or watch your children spill a bowl of cereal all over the floor you might want to think about this: The average dairy cow produces about 100 pounds of milk a day. It should also be noted that a cow also produces about 30 pounds of urine and 65 pounds of manure each day, as well as about 200 pounds of flatulence. You might say that dairy cows are walking factories, constantly producing all manner of liquids, solids, and gasses.

Cows in general occupy a unique place in human history. They have been considered one of the oldest forms of wealth— worth their weight in gold or brides, depending on which you considered to be more valuable. Indeed, they have been traded, purchased, and stolen ever since the dawn of recorded history. They've been illustrated on cave walls and celebrated in story and song. Their importance to humans may be due simply to the incredible variety of usable products they supply. Cows give us milk, cheese, other dairy products, meat, and leather for clothing and protection. In the 1800s, people traveling in wagon trains across the Midwest would burn dried cow dung in lieu of wood. And throughout history, cows have been used as beasts of burden to pull carts, plow fields, and carry loads. Currently, there are about 1.3 billion head of cattle in the world— over 200 million in India, where they are considered sacred.

It is the ubiquitous dairy cow that we celebrate here. Were you aware that a dairy cow will spend approximately six hours a day feeding? During that time, it will take in about 100 pounds of food and drink between 25 to 50 gallons of water. Each cow then spends more than eight hours a day chewing its cud—regurgitated, partially digested food (grass is mostly cellulose, difficult for many animals, including cows, to digest; this is one reason why they must eat so much of it).

After the cud is chewed, the material passes through the cow's four stomachs: the rumen, reticulum, omasum, and adomasum. The rumen is the largest stomach and acts as a fermentation chamber. The abomasum is the last of the four and is comparable in both structure and function to the human stomach.

The age of a cow can be determined by its teeth and its horns. Like humans, cows get permanent molars at different times of their lives. The temporary "baby" teeth begin to fall out when the cow is 21 months old and are entirely replaced by permanent teeth when the cow is 4. On its horns, there's one ring for each year of life.

The average life span of a dairy cow is 7 years. The oldest cow on record is a Dremon cow named Big Bertha who died 3 months shy of age 49, on New Year's Eve 1993. Big Bertha holds the record for lifetime breeding, producing thirty-nine calves. During her life, Big Bertha also produced:

- 480 tons of manure
- 525,600 pounds of urine
- 2,000,000 pounds of saliva
- 3,500,000 pounds of gas

Way to go, Big Bertha!

GOLDFISH

49 years

Do you remember going to a county fair or school carnival and tossing a handful of ping-pong balls at a cluster of goldfish bowls? Each bowl held a small fish that must have wondered why people were trying to throw small objects into its already-cramped living space. Occasionally, some lucky individual would, through sheer luck and a complete defiance of the laws of physics, toss a ball into a bowl. The concessionaire would then pour the bowl's fish and tepid water into a long plastic bag, and the lucky winner would take the keepsake home, where the creature would bear the moniker Goldy or Lucky or Fred. Unfortunately, and most tragically, the small, golden fish was usually doomed to a life that was, at best, a mere 4 to 5 weeks in duration.

Certainly one of the most well-known of all fish, goldfish have been around since the earliest Chinese dynasties. They were introduced to Europe in the late seventeenth century. Since then, goldfish have become one of the most popular domesticated pets. They are small, inexpensive, and hardy (except when confined to small bowls). There are more than two dozen varieties raised by fish fanciers in ponds and aquariums throughout the world.

While most people probably believe that all goldfish are destined for but a brief stay upon this earth, such is not the case. Goldfish will, with proper care, feeding, and aerated water, live up to 10 years in captivity. Interestingly, a large percentage of goldfish succumb when people touch them. Goldfish, like many other species of fish, are covered by a protective slime that prevents waterborne bacteria and parasites from getting to their skin and eventually into their systems. Touching the fish removes a portion of that protective layer, and the creature often dies as a result. The other obstacle to a long goldfish life is the buildup of toxic wastes in the water, something that occurs with relative frequency in the cramped confines of small aquaria or diminutive ponds.

There is one goldfish that has defied the odds, however. This rare individual, through a little environmental luck and the great care of its keeper, was able to live for 49 years. Its life span was considerably enhanced with a carefully and painstakingly balanced diet, consisting of a low level of protein and a high level of carbohydrates. Goldfish enthusiasts (particularly in Asia) will sometimes supplement a fish's diet with shelled peas and green, leafy vegetables and live food such as water fleas and bloodworms. Brine shrimp are often fed to young goldfish to stimulate growth.

SUNDEW

50 years

Have you ever been attacked by a piece of celery or a bunch of lima beans? Have you ever been eaten by a fruit tree or berry patch? In your nightmares, perhaps—those wild imaginings you never tell anybody about.

There are, in fact, several plants whose survival is dependent upon the consumption of animals—six hundred species of carnivorous plants known for capturing small creatures, typically insects. How does this work? Usually an insect lands on a particular surface of one of these plants where it is immobilized by a specialized trap, some type of sticky substance, or a deadly liquid. The unfortunate creature is then soaked in a variety of juices, dissolved, and absorbed into the plant's system. Nutrients (primarily nitrogen) from the creature's body are used to nourish the plant.

Over the millennia, carnivorous plants have developed special "tools" that allow them to survive in nutrient-poor conditions. This is an example of selective adaptation—when a species develops characteristics that allow it to compensate for a specific environmental deficiency. Since there is little or no nitrogen in the soil where these plants typically live, they must obtain that necessary nutrient from another source—in this case, insects.

One of the smallest members of the plant kingdom is also one of the most violent: the sundew. There are more than 180 varieties of sundews throughout the world, ranging in size from 1 inch across to nearly 1 foot or more in height. Sundews have been known to achieve a life span of 50 years, but they are most noted for clusters of small, brightly colored leaves growing around the base of their stems. Each leaf is covered by 400 or so hairlike bristles (aficionados of carnivorous plants—and you know who you are—prefer to call these "tentacles"). These bristles get progressively larger as they radiate out to the edges of the leaves. But it is what is on these bristles that is so amazing.

Each bristle is tipped with a drop of sticky fluid produced by glands inside the plant. From a distance, the plant appears to be covered with droplets of dew glistening in the sun (hence the name). Insects, particularly flying ones, are attracted to these brilliant droplets. When an insect lands on a sundew leaf, it quickly becomes stuck, and as it struggles, it coats its body with more and more of the sticky fluid. Eventually, the helpless insect is completely covered with the stuff and dies.

The insect's struggles stimulate the outer hairs on the leaf to curl inward, further ensnaring the prey. In some sundew species, the bristle motion is extremely fast—some of the glands can bend 180 degrees in just a fraction of a second. As the leaf curls inward, it continues to release powerful digestive juices that slowly eat away at the now-dead creature. These juices eventually digest all the insect's soft tissues, which are slowly absorbed by the hairs on the sundew's leaves.

It usually takes about one week for an insect to be completely absorbed. Afterward, the leaves open slowly, and the trap is reset. All that remains is the outer skeleton of the victim. Of course the nagging question is: If there were a carnivorous plant big enough, would it be able to digest human flesh? Who would you want to test this on?

STEGOSAURUS

50 years

This dinosaur's name means "roofed lizard" and comes from its most distinguishing feature: the double row of seventeen tall, triangular plates rising from its neck, back, and tail. (O. C. Marsh, who originally named the creature, mistakenly believed that the dermal plates overlaid each other, much like the shingles on a roof.)

These plates rose from the surface of the skin, not from the skeleton, and their function has never been clear. Original theories suggested that they were used primarily for defense, protecting the animal from attacks by large predators. This theory has largely been discounted, yet modern-day paleontologists still can't agree on a new one. One idea is that because the plates had blood vessels running through them they helped control body temperature. Other researchers suggest that the plates were used to intimidate enemies by making the *Stegosaurus* look larger than it was. Still others suggest that they were used in some form of sexual display.

An average adult *Stegosaurus* reached a length of about 25 feet and weighed a little more than 5 tons. This would have made it equivalent to a modern-day minke whale. It was also distinguished by an arched back that tapered at one end to a tail and at the other end to a seemingly undersized head. The head was held low to the ground, an obvious advantage for an herbivorous dinosaur. The *Stegosaurus* also possessed a toothless beak at the front of its mouth that it used to tear vegetation. With a little imagination, one can see the creature as a small-headed elephant with severely shortened legs. It is spec-ulated that it had a voracious appetite, feasting primarily on conifers, cycads, horsetails, ferns, and mosses. Like modern-day birds and crocodiles, it swallowed gastroliths to help it process its food.

Scientists have been puzzled by the *Stegosaurus'* skull, which is very small in proportion to the rest of its body. It also had an extremely small brain—about the size of a golf ball. While the overall weight of the *Stegosaurus* was more than 5 tons, its brain was a mere 2.8 ounces, making a ratio of body-weight to brain-weight of 57,142 to 1.

Determining how long these creatures lived is also a puzzle for paleontologists. Recently, scientists have discovered that many dinosaur bones have growth rings similar to the growth rings in trees. Each year of growth leaves a faint trace in the bone. Estimates of life spans can also be calculated based on body size and the fact that large animals generally live longer than smaller ones. As a result, it has been estimated that huge *Sauropods* might have lived for 50 years or more, and so it seems possible that the *Stegosaurus* might have matched these Late Jurassic dinosaurs.

GORILLA

55 + years

When discussing gorillas, there is a high level of disagreement among zoologists about the exact number of subspecies. Both the Smithsonian Institution and the World Wildlife Fund list two species (eastern gorilla and western gorilla) and four subspecies. Other sources list five subspecies. We'll go with the Smithsonian.

Probably the best-known of all gorillas, the mountain gorilla is the one most often seen in nature programs and books. Mountain gorillas live on the slopes of the Virunga Volcanoes in a small area of Africa where Zaire, Uganda, and Rwanda meet. They are called mountain gorillas simply because their habitat is between 9,000 and 12,000 feet in elevation. Unfortunately, because of poaching and illegal hunting, their numbers have been reduced so much that there are today only about three hundred left in the wild.

Another well-known gorilla is the western lowland gorilla, which lives throughout Cameroon, Gabon, Central African Republic, and Congo. This subspecies lives in coastal rain forests from sea level up to about 6,000 feet above sea level. A third subspecies is the eastern lowland gorilla, which inhabits the deep jungles of Zaire. It lives in rain forests from sea level to about 8,000 feet. The fourth subspecies, the Cross River gorilla, can be found on the border between Cameroon and Nigeria. It's considered one of the twenty-five most endangered primates in the world—only about 250 to 300 remain in the wild.

A gorilla's diet consists primarily of leaves, branches, grasses, shrubs, and tree bark. Lowland gorillas also eat fruits, such as bananas and mangos, when they are available. Gorillas typically eat almost all day long. In fact, a large gorilla may eat as much as 70 pounds of food a day (you and I, on the other hand, only eat about 2 pounds of food a day).

The life span of gorillas is difficult to determine because of their isolation and endangered status. Most primatologists agree that a range of 30 to 35 years in the wild seems about right. In captivity, gorillas will often live to age 50. The world record holder appears to be a gorilla in the Dallas Zoo named Jenny. She passed away from an inoperable stomach tumor at 55.4 years of age.

HORSE

62 years

The earliest ancestor of the horse was eohippus, the "dawn horse," which lived about fifty-five million years ago in what is now North America and Europe. The creature, which stood no higher than 15 inches, looked more like a greyhound than any horse we would recognize.

Modern horses were first brought to the New World by the Vikings in the early 1000s. A little more than five hundred years later, Spanish explorers brought horses with them to Mexico. Some of these horses escaped and became wild; their descendants were eventually tamed by Native Americans. The offspring of the feral horses, sometimes called mustangs, once roamed the western plains in herds that numbered into the millions.

Today, the world's horse population is estimated at seventy-five million. China not only has the most people on the planet, it also has the most horses—some ten million. Currently, there are more than 350 different breeds of horses and ponies throughout the world.

Horses have an average life span of between 20 and 25 years; some can live to be over 30. You can tell the age of a horse by its teeth. A horse usually gets all of its teeth by the time it is 5. After that, the teeth grow longer with each passing year.

One particular horse had lots of care and excellent teeth and lived to the age of 62. Known as Old Billy, he was a barge horse owned by Mersey and Irwell Navigation in England in the late 1700s and early 1800s. During that time, horse-drawn barges were used to transport cargo along canals. Barge horses became obsolete with the onset of the Industrial Revolution and the invention of the boat engine.

Old Billy was born in Woolston, in Lancashire County, in 1760. He died on November 27, 1822. In the Warrington Museum, there is a lithograph of Old Billy and his owner made when the horse was 59. Also enshrined in the museum is Old Billy's head.

Here are some additional horse facts:

- If a statue of a mounted warrior shows the horse with both front feet in the air, the warrior died in battle. If the horse has one front foot in the air, the person died as a result of wounds received in battle. If the horse has all four feet on the ground, the person died of natural causes.
- One horsepower equals 746 watts.
- Horses cannot breathe through their mouths.
- Discoveries at the city of Susa in southwestern Asia indicate that horses were probably tamed and ridden about 5,000 years ago.
- A horse is considered an adult at age 4.
- Horses were initially used as a source of meat.
- Horses can drink up to ten gallons of water a day.
- Horses are measured in hands; a hand is 4 inches.
- Horses have two blind spots: One is directly behind them, the other directly in front of them.

OSTRICH

75 years

Ostriches are members of a group known as flightless birds, which also includes Australian emus, New Guinea cassowaries, and New Zealand kiwis. These birds make up less than 1 percent of all the birds in the world.

The ostrich, like its other flightless relatives, has lost the strong, stiff feathers of the wing and tail that mark aerial species. Instead, a growth of soft plumage acts as insulation against the harsh temperatures endured by ostriches throughout their arid range. The ostrich's wings are very small, with 2 of the wing "fingers" ending in claws or spurs that can be used as weapons.

Ostriches are the world's tallest birds. An adult male will stand nearly 8 feet high and weigh between 140 and 230 pounds. In spite of their size, these birds are fast runners. An ostrich has been observed passing an antelope at full gallop, traveling 40 mph, which places it among the fastest of all birds. They will often cruise along at a steady 30 mph over long stretches. Newborn chicks can run soon after they hatch. In a month, they can hit speeds of 35 mph, easily besting any Olympic sprinter.

When ostriches are chased by other animals, they don't run away. They run in circles. If caught, ostriches fight with their feet, which have two strong toes. The longest toe on each foot is armed with a sharp claw that can inflict major damage to an enemy.

In the wild, ostriches mingle with other animals, such as zebras and antelopes, which kick up insects and other small critters that ostriches eat. Because ostriches are so tall, they can see approaching enemies and sound an alarm for their companions. It's a mutually beneficial situation.

Female ostriches lay six to eight eggs at one time. Each of these is about 6 inches long and can weigh 5 pounds. The eggs are almost spherical in shape. During the day, the female sits on the eggs; at night, the male does the incubating.

After hatching, baby ostriches grow rapidly, reaching a height of 6 feet in 6 months. The parents are protective of their young, leading them to food, water, and protection. Even so, only about one in ten chicks survives the first year of life. Chicks mature at about 4 years and can have a life span of from 30 years (in the wild) to a maximum of 75 (in captivity).

Ostriches are found mainly in central and southern Africa. They live in dry areas and often travel in large groups. In desert areas, they get their water by eating succulent plants. They also eat stones and pebbles to help them digest food. Many herbivorous dinosaurs did the same thing, lending further weight to the idea that dinosaurs and birds are closely related.

Despite what many people think, ostriches do not hide their heads in the sand.

ALLIGATOR

75 years

Don't know the difference between an alligator and a crocodile? The following will come in handy: An alligator's head is flat and broad; a crocodile's is narrow and pointed. An alligator's snout is U-shaped; a crocodile's is V-shaped. An alligator keeps all its short teeth in its mouth when it's closed; two of the crocodile's long, sharp bottom teeth stick out of its mouth when it's closed. An alligator's skin is blackish, green, or blue-gray; a crocodile's is olive or gray-green.

The name alligator is an anglicized form of the Spanish *el lagarto* (meaning lizard), which early Spanish explorers and settlers in Florida called the fearsome creature. There are two alligator species: the American alligator (*Alligator mississippiensis*) in the southeastern part of the country, mostly in Florida and Louisiana, and the much smaller Chinese alligator (*Alligator sinensis*), found along the Yangtze River. (The Asian species is considered endangered, with few individuals left in the wild.) Some scientists refer to the alligator as a living fossil because it has survived for more than 150 million years, far outlasting its cousin, the dinosaur.

An American alligator, on average, will reach a weight of 1,000 pounds and a length of 15 feet. Its life span averages between 35 and 50 years in the wild. Predation, habitat reduction, and a demand for alligator products tend to have a negative impact on the longevity of alligators.

The current record for longest-lived American alligator is held by Cabulitis, who lived in the Riga Zoo in Latvia. When he died, in 2007, he was more than 75 years old.

In Latvian, *cabulitis* roughly translates as "sweet and tender creature." Zookeepers reported that during the last years of his life, Cabulitis enjoyed being sprayed with warm water and having his back brushed (who doesn't?). He was also particularly fond of German pop music and would roar with approval whenever it was played.

ELEPHANT
86 years

Those of you who spend a great deal of time walking in high heels will appreciate an animal that walks on its tiptoes. Behind an elephant's toes is a thick pad, a tough section of connective tissue that functions as a sole. When an elephant walks, it uses the typical walking pattern of most large mammals: heel strike and toe off. This results in the weight of an elephant's forelimbs resting more on the tip of each toe than on the soles, similar to someone walking in a pair of 3-inch heels. A 7-ton elephant can walk (or tiptoe) noiselessly through the forest or across the savanna.

There are two species of elephants. The African elephant, which lives in central and southern Africa, is the world's largest land animal. An African bull can weigh up to 15,000 pounds, about the weight of a school bus. Cows are considerably smaller. A full-grown African elephant stands 13 feet tall at the shoulder and has enormous ears that can be 6 feet from top to bottom. If you look closely, you might notice that the ears resemble the outline of Africa.

The Asian elephant, which lives in India and several south-east Asia countries, is smaller than its African relative. An adult Asian bull can weigh up to 6 tons and stand 10 feet tall. Asian elephants have much smaller ears than do African elephants, and some people say that their ears are similar in shape to an outline of India. Asian elephants are distinguished by two bumps on the top of their heads; African elephants have only one bump. Most circuses and zoos have Asian elephants.

Elephants usually live together in two different types of herds. Adult bulls spend most of their time alone or with other bulls. Cows and calves live in their own herds, separate from the males except at mating time. Cow and calf herds are always led by an older female known as the matriarch, who is responsible for the group's safety and helping it find water and food.

Adult elephants can suffer a range of ailments similar to those experienced by humans: cardiovascular problems, arthritis, and post-reproductive symptoms similar to menopause.

The average life span of an elephant is about 70 years. An elephant named Lin Wang that lived in Taipei's Muzha Zoo reached age 86 before eventually succumbing to severe arthritis in February 2003.

DIPLODOCUS

100 years

Diplodocus was a common dinosaur during the Late Jurassic Period (161 to 145 million years ago). Its name means "double beam," in reference to T-shaped bones in its tail. It was one of the larger dinosaurs of the period, measuring up to 90 feet long—26 feet of that length was its neck, and another 45 feet was the tail. For a long time, it was known as the world's largest land creature. Not until the discovery of *Supersaurus* was *Diplodocus* changed from "the longest" to "one of the longest."

The image of *Diplodocus* is familiar to most people, perhaps because so many *Diplodocus* skeletons have been unearthed and placed in museums around the world, including the Natural History Museum of London, the Field Museum of Natural History in Chicago, the Senchenberg Museum in Germany, and the Natural Science Museum in Spain. *Diplodocus* has also been featured in numerous dinosaur movies, is a usual part of dinosaur toys and games, and was "novelized" in James Michener's *Centennial*. It lived throughout what is now western North America. Its remains have been uncovered in Colorado, Utah, Wyoming, and Montana.

Despite its mass, *Diplodocus* was more lightly built than other Sauropods, weighing a mere 10 to 20 tons. Its forelimbs were slightly shorter than its hind limbs, resulting in a posture that was more-or-less horizontal. Its neck may have been used to poke into forests to get foliage that was otherwise unavailable to the bulky Sauropods that couldn't venture into woodlands because of their size. One recent study, however, suggests that the primary function of the neck was for sexual display.

The first *Diplodocus* fossil was found at Como Bluff, Wyoming, in 1878. Fossils of the dinosaur are common at many digs in the Rocky Mountains—with the exception of the skull, which is often missing from otherwise complete skeletons.

Studies of the bones reveal that *Diplodocus* grew at a fast rate, often reaching maturity at about age 10. Growth seems to have been constant throughout the dinosaur's life. Some scientists have estimated the maximum life span at about 100 years, although that number is open to dispute.

HUMAN

122 years, 164 days

I suppose that if you wanted to do a psychological study on humans' predisposition to lie, fib, and otherwise perjure themselves you could begin by simply asking them their age. Ever since the advent of movie ratings, youngsters have looked ticket-takers straight in the eye and calmly added a few years to their ages. At cocktail parties, legions of singles have either added or subtracted years depending on who was standing next to them. And a few of us have casually over-stated things a bit to get an additional 10 percent discount at the supermarket.

In fact, fibbing about age has probably been taking place in every century and civilization since the dawn of history. Stories about legendary centenarians, age-defying potions, and eternal retirement spots have been passed down through scores of gen-erations ever since humans invented speech.

In ancient times, longevity stories were created as an ele-ment of religious beliefs. The longer humans lived (or thought they should live), the more connected they were to the spirits of their ancestors. As the stories were passed down from one generation to the next, a few years were added here and there to extend a genealogy further back into the past. In Japan, the ages of emperors were inflated in an attempt to extend Japanese history well beyond that of Europeans. The ancient Romans, always eager to demonstrate their superiority, fre-quently proclaimed longevity examples like that of Nestor, who allegedly lived for 300 years, or Tirasis of Thebes, who supposedly lived well into his 600s. Currently, throughout the world, the average life expectancy of all humans is 67 years. This ranges from a low of 31.99 years in Swaziland to a high of 84.33 years in Macau.

In many primeval cultures, old people were a rarity, and when a village elder did exceed the norm he or she was revered and celebrated—in song, dance, and story. Quite naturally, tales would evolve about how they achieved a long life—stories that were spiced up to outdo the tales of neighboring villages. Since most stories from the countryside were shared as part of the oral tradition, facts were of small consequence, and ages of 150 and 160 years were often reported (though never verified) for the respected oldsters.

Many of the claims of longevity come from regions in which record keeping was poor (or in which fibbing was an art). The lack of birth certificates and the tendency of individuals to alter their birth dates have led to many an unsubstantiated story. One of the most extreme cases in the 20th century was a 1933 wire story announcing that China's Li Chung Yun, born in 1680, had died at age 256 (apparently the reporter's math skills were slightly askew, for if the birth date were true, Mr. Yun actually would have been 252 or 253).

It wasn't until 20th-century science became obsessed with accuracy that the question of human longevity or lack thereof was finally subjected to logical analysis. To validate an individual's longevity claim requires a detailed investigation of records, beginning with an official birth certificate in combination with additional documents recording selected events in the person's life. Although there are many supposed candidates, the undisputed claim for the world's oldest human being belongs to a Frenchwoman, Jeanne Calment, born on February 21, 1875, in Arles. She passed away on August 4,

1997, aged 122 years, 164 days. Her life span has been thoroughly documented, and more records have been produced to verify her age than for any other case.

Ms. Calment outlived her husband by 55 years and her only child by 63. She took up fencing at 85, rode a bicycle until she reached 100, was able to walk until she was almost 115, quit smoking when she was 117, and consumed chocolates until the age of 119. She lived on her own until the age of 110, when she was moved into a nursing home. During her life, she attended the funeral of Victor Hugo, in 1885, and met Vincent van Gogh when she was 14. (In 1990, she appeared briefly in the film *Vincent and Me*, making her the oldest movie actress ever, at 115 years.)

Calment came from a family consisting of several individuals who lived to ripe old ages. Her brother lived to be 97, her father 93, and her mother 86.

During an interview given when she was in her 120s, Calment was asked about the secret of her longevity. She attributed her extended years to olive oil, which she said she poured on all her food and rubbed into her skin. She was also quoted as saying, "I've only got one wrinkle, and I'm sitting on it."

LOBSTER

140 years

This is the story of George, whom some may call the world's most fortunate lobster, but whom we'll just call the oldest marine crustacean. Before we get to George's story, however, we should first deal with the story of lobsters in general.

Now considered a delicacy, the lobster was not always in favor as an epicurean delight. Prior to the mid-19th century, eating lobster was considered a mark of poverty. In fact, sometime before the Revolutionary War, dock workers in Boston went on strike to protest the fact that they had to eat lobster more than three times a week (oh, the things those dock workers had to endure). It was the development of the modern transportation system (and perhaps the invention of melted butter) that changed the fate of the lowly lobster forever. Improved modes of transport meant that lobsters could be shipped fresh to the big cites of New York and Philadelphia. As a result, they became a luxury food . . . as well as a reason for folks to visit overpriced resorts throughout Maine.

Lobsters can be found all along the continental shelf, typically living in crevices and under rocks. They have a hard exoskeleton and, like other arthropods, must undergo a regular molting process. Lobsters typically feed on fish, mollusks, other crustaceans, worms, and a variety of plant life. Unlike you and me, lobsters grow continuously throughout their lives. Assuming they are not captured, they may live to be 100 or older.

Back to George: George lived a contented life sequestered in a large aquarium at City Crab and Seafood Restaurant in New York City. Diners would come in and stare at him, and George would do what lobsters always do, which is pretty much just sit there and stare back. The manager of the restaurant once remarked that George spent most of his time "sitting in the restaurant's tank and acting as a sort of mascot."

The manager calculated that George was around 140 years old. Lobsters can grow 1 pound every 7 to 10 years, and since George was about 18 or 20 pounds, it seemed reasonable to infer that George was approximately 14 decades old. (In case you are wondering, George was not the heaviest lobster on record. That distinction belongs to a gargantuan specimen caught off Nova Scotia that weighed 44.4 pounds.)

One day, while George was living his quiet existence, some kind-hearted folks came along and said that the creature lacked both space and excitement. They complained that George should be out in the ocean with his own kind. And so George was packed up and transported to Maine, where he was rather unceremoniously dumped into the chilly waters somewhere along the coast.

For all we know, he might still be there, creeping along the sea bottom and molting to his aged heart's content.

TORTOISE

188 years

Ask most people to name the oldest living creatures on earth and they will probably nominate the tortoise. The creature's slow and deliberate lifestyle (it travels at a speed of about 0.16 mph), a tendency to relax in the sun and wallow in mud puddles, and a careful and systematic ingestion of food contribute to the perception that the tortoise's life span is quite long.

This persistent perception has spawned all sorts of false tales and erroneous reports. Most of these stories suffer from misinformation and inaccurate record-keeping, but they are no less colorful as a result.

But there are some frequently cited and scientifically authenticated records of longevity for these creatures.

- Tu'i Malila was the name of a Madagascar radiated tortoise given to the royal family of Tonga by Captain James Cook. It was born around 1777, and when it died, in May 1965, it was estimated to have lived for 188 years.
- Jonathan is a Seychelles giant tortoise living on the island of St. Helena. He was brought there with several other tortoises in 1882, when he was approximately 50 years old, and is still alive today. At present, he is more than 177 years old.
- Reportedly collected by Charles Darwin on his voyage to the Galapagos Islands in 1835, Harriet was a Galapagos tortoise that had an estimated age of 175 years when she

died, in Australia, in June 2006, of heart failure. (A bit of trivia: *Galapagos* actually means "tortoise" in Spanish.)

- Timothy was a Mediterranean spur-thighed tortoise who served as a mascot on a number of British ships throughout the late 1880s. Originally believed to be a male, it was only when the creature was about 87 years old that it was discovered that he was actually a she. Timothy lived to be approximately 165 years old. She died in April 2004.

Documenting the age of tortoises has always been a challenge. Scientists who require authentication often come up against the general public and popular press, which may be somewhat inclined to add a year—or a decade—here and there to make things more interesting. Suffice it to say that even though tortoises have established themselves as one of the longest-lived creatures in the world, they are not even the longest-lived vertebrate. More on this later.

SAGUARO CACTUS
200 years

This iconic inhabitant of the Sonoran Desert is a botanical species with a few features many of us might envy— it stands tall and robust, is able to withstand temperature extremes, is popular with its neighbors, and is universally recognized. Of course, it is also a bit prickly, but let's not quibble about minor details.

The saguaro (pronounced sah-WAH-roh) lives exclusively in an area encompassing southeastern California, southern Arizona, and northwestern Mexico. It provides food, shelter, and moisture for a variety of desert animals, including rattlesnakes, gila monsters, bats, owls, scorpions, and rats. Some of these creatures live around the saguaro, while others live inside the desert giant. Saguaros thrive in rocky areas and desert slopes from sea level up to 4,500 feet in elevation. They require very little water and can often survive two years without rain.

The saguaro has a root system that is shallow and wide-reaching. Each plant is supported by a tap root, which is basically a pad about 3 feet long. Other roots go no deeper than a foot into the ground yet radiate out from the base to a distance equal to the height of the plant. This allows for quick absorption of water during infrequent showers. The roots also wrap around rocks, providing anchorage against the winds that frequently whip across the desert.

Saguaros can grow as tall as 56 feet and weigh as much as 6 tons. Even though the saguaro lives in an arid environment, about 75 to 95 percent of its overall weight is water. Its most distinguishing features—its arms—don't begin to grow until the plant is between 50 and 70 years old. An average saguaro will have five arms.

From May to June, a couple hundred large, white, waxy flowers blossom on a full-grown saguaro. Clustered near the ends of branches, the blossoms contain nectar that attracts birds and bats. Each flower opens once during a cool desert night and closes again by next midday—never to open again. Open flowers allow particular species such as the lesser long-nose bat and Mexican long-tongue bat to pollinate the plant. Out of the forty million seeds a saguaro will produce in its lifetime, only one will likely develop into a plant that outlives its parent. Disease, drought, and temperature extremes, including winter cold, kill off most saguaro seedlings before they reach maturity.

The skin of a saguaro is smooth and waxy and protects the interior of the plant from the penetrating rays of the sun, preventing valuable moisture from evaporating. The trunk and stems of a mature saguaro have stout, 2-inch spines clustered on the ribs. When water is absorbed, the outer pulp of the saguaro can expand like an accordion, increasing the diameter of the stem and increasing the plant's weight by up to a ton. Birds such as the gila woodpecker and gilded flicker make their homes in the saguaro by chiseling out small holes in the trunk.

The saguaro grows extremely slowly—its growth rate is measured in fractions of an inch per year. A 10-year-old saguaro is less than 2 inches tall. By 50 to 70 years of age, most saguaros reach a height of approximately 10 feet and begin to grow arms. Saguaros are considered mature when they reach an age of 125 years. The tallest and oldest saguaros may grow as high as 50 feet. They have an average life span of between 150 to 175 years, although 200-year-old specimens are not unknown.

ROUGHEYE ROCKFISH

205 years

H ere's a creature that proves you don't have to be pretty to live a long life. The rougheye rockfish looks like it's from a 1950s science fiction movie. Its weird eyes give it its name; the creature sports two to ten spines along the lower rims of its eyes (some rougheyes lack the namesake appendages).

The rougheye rockfish has an expansive range that extends from San Diego to the Aleutian Islands and the Bering Sea to the Kamchatka Peninsula and Japan. Most of the population lives along the continental shelf at depths ranging from 80 to over 9,000 feet. For unknown reasons, adults tend to inhabit deeper regions than do the younger fish. It has recently been discovered that rougheyes probably comprise two distinct species with possibly different depth distributions. The types (known simply as type I and type II) have similar appearances with just slight variations in color. It's known that smaller rougheyes tend to congregate in large schools while larger fish prefer solitude or small groups. This grouping behavior seems to occur mostly in the fall and winter months and might coincide with the mating season.

Fishing for rougheyes is an important industry off the western coast of Canada, the Pacific Northwest, and Japan.

Rougheyes may be among the longest-lived marine fishes on earth. One specimen caught in Alaska was determined to have reached the age of 205 years. Caleb Finch, a scientist at the University of Southern California, has coined the term "negligible senescence" to describe very slow or negligible aging in select species of animals. His criteria for negligible aging include "no observable age-related increase in mortality rate or decrease in reproduction rate after maturity." He has listed several creatures with this characteristic, including the rockfish, as well as the sturgeon, some turtles and bivalves, and lobsters.

BOWHEAD WHALE

211 years

The bowhead whale is distinguished by a large, bow-shaped head that is up to 40 percent of its body length. Bowheads are part of a group known as baleen whales; they feed on plankton and tiny crustaceans, like krill, copepods, and pteropods, from Arctic waters, where they live year-round. The arched mouth of a bowhead is enormous, up to 10 feet wide and 20 feet deep. The whales use their mouths like skimmers, slowly swimming through shoals or schools of food with their mouths open, using fine hairs to filter out tiny prey. Bowheads will occasionally poke around in the mud on the ocean floor to stir up any critters they miss.

Bowheads grow to 60 feet in length (which would make the head about 24 feet long). At birth, they weigh about 1 ton and eventually grow to more than 60 tons as adults. They are well insulated with blubber, which can be up to 20 inches thick in places. A bowhead's head is protected by heavy skull bones that allow the whale to break through heavy ice in order to breathe. It appears as though bowheads use a form of echolocation in order to determine the thickness of the ice above them.

Once while helping an Alaskan native whale-hunter cut blubber from a killed bowhead whale, biologist Craig George pressed his knife into a deep scar in the whale's skin and it made a crunching noise. He cut deeper, and, moments later, pulled out an old but still-sharp harpoon point the whale had been carrying for perhaps a century. George contacted Jeffrey

Bada, a geochemist who determines the age of living things by studying changes in levels of aspartic acid, an amino acid found in the eye lenses and teeth of animals. As a result of his analysis, Bada concluded that the whale was 211 years old at the time of its death. He explained that the method he used has an accuracy range of about 16 percent, which means the bowhead could have been anywhere between 177 and 245 years old, but that the 211-year-old estimate was probably the most accurate. That particular whale, alive when Bill Clinton was president, was also swimming in Arctic waters when Thomas Jefferson was elected.

KOI

226 years

O riginally found throughout Central Europe and Asia, the fish known as koi (or "brocaded carp") have been raised and admired for centuries. First domesticated in China and southeast Asia and bred in Japan in the 1820s for stunning coloration, koi come in a rainbow of colors: white, black, red, yellow, blue, and cream. Raising koi is still a popular hobby in Japan, with some varieties worth hundreds or even thousands of dollars.

Koi are often confused with goldfish, and both were originally developed from carp (koi are the domesticated version of the common carp, while goldfish were bred from Prussian carp). Goldfish have a much greater variety of body shapes, tail and fin configurations, and sizes than koi do. In general, goldfish are also considerably smaller. Koi, on the other hand, have a much wider range of colors. Koi and goldfish (and carp, for that matter) can adapt to many different climates and a broad range of water conditions.

Most koi can live for decades, often as long as their owners. One particular koi, however, has the distinction of being authenticated as the oldest living vertebrate in recorded history. When Hanako died on July 7, 1977, she had reached the age of 226.

Hanako's age was determined by a process similar to dentrochronology, the science of counting tree rings in order to determine the age of a tree. Tree rings are the result of new growth in the vascular cambium layer of a tree. Visible rings result from the change in growth speed through the seasons of the year, so one ring usually marks the passage of one year in the life of the tree. Fish also produce growth rings on each of their scales: One ring is produced for each year a fish has been alive. By counting the number of growth rings on a single fish scale, scientists can determine the exact age of the creature. In 1966, 10 years before her death, one of Hanako's scales was carefully removed and studied. A scale-ring count revealed that she was 216 years old at that time. When she died, her age could be easily verified.

QUAHOG CLAM

405 years

Imagine being around when Shakespeare was writing his comedies. Or when the English were establishing colonies in the Americas. Or when Galileo was being tried for advocating that the earth revolved around the sun.

In 2007, a team of scientists was conducting research as part of a long-term project to understand how the world's climate has changed over the past thousand years. While anchored off the frigid northern coast of Iceland, they pulled up what may be the oldest animal on record: a Quahog clam. When investigators at Bangor University in England counted the clam's growth rings (similar to the growth rings in trees) they came up with a life span of 405 years. The clam, which unfortunately died during the ring-counting procedure, was nicknamed Ming after the Chinese dynasty that ruled when the clam "settled" (the mollusk equivalent of being born).

The clam's demise was for a good cause. The researchers hope to use shell studies to reconstruct a record of environmental changes over the past several centuries. Al Wanamaker, a team member, explained, "Just like tree rings, those growth lines vary in accordance with the environment." Shell growth is related to water temperature, salinity, and food availability, for example.

Quahog clams are known among marine biologists as some of the longest-living animals on the planet. Previous to the discovery of this quadricentenarian, the record for the oldest animal was held by a 374-year-old Icelandic quahog clam housed in a German museum. According to the *Guinness Book of World Records*, the oldest American creature is a 220-year-old clam taken in 1982.

If you want to live a long life, it doesn't hurt to be a mollusk.

SAW PALMETTO

700 years

Consider a small palm tree that grows wild from Texas all the way across the Deep South to South Carolina. This plant—the saw palmetto—gets its name from the spiny, sawtoothed stems that lie at the base of each leaf. And with a life span of up to 700 years, the plant seems almost indestructible, resisting drought, insect infestation, and fire.

The saw palmetto's much-touted medicinal properties are derived from its blue-black berries, which are usually harvested in August and September. (This process is sometimes hazardous, however; harvesters can easily be cut by the razor-sharp leaf stems, and they also risk being bitten by the diamondback rattlesnakes that often make their homes in the shade of this scrubby palm. The cure, it seems, might be more dangerous than the disease.)

For quite some time, the saw palmetto has had a reputation as an aphrodisiac. Over the years, it has been used by doctors in Italy, Germany, and France to reduce noncancerous enlarged prostate glands, strengthen and tone the male reproductive system, and increase libido. The herb is not only helpful in maintaining a proper hormone balance in the prostate, it also provides sterols and fatty acids that inhibit inflammation. It should come as no surprise, then, that this herb is now one of the ten best-selling nutritional supplements in the United States.

This is nothing new. The saw palmetto has had a long history of folk use. Native Americans valued it for treating disorders of the urinary tract. Early American colonists, noting the vitality of animals who fed on the berries, used the fruits as a general tonic, particularly for the frail or elderly. It's also been used to improve digestion.

SACRED FIG

2,259 + years

Imagine a plant that was alive since before the rise of the Roman Empire, the building of Chichen Itza in Mexico, and the rule of the Ming Dynasty. Hard to believe? Today, in Sri Lanka, lives a tree that was first planted in 249 B.C., making it about 2,260 years old. And it's still growing.

The sacred fig (*Ficus religiosa*) is a species of banyan fig native to India, Nepal, Sri Lanka, southwest China, and Indochina east to Vietnam. It's known by a wide range of common names, depending on the country and language. In Burmese, it's *bo, pou, bawdi*, or *bawdi nyaung*. In Thai, it's *pipal, arasa maram*, or the *ashvastha* tree. The fact that banyan trees have been around for so long may be one reason why they have been given so many different names by so many different groups of people.

The sacred fig is a large, dry-season, deciduous (or semi-evergreen) tree. It can grow to 90 feet high, and its trunk can measure up to 10 feet in diameter. Its leaves are long and broad with a distinctive extended tip. The fruit of the tree is a small green fig, 1/2 inch in diameter, that becomes purple as it ripens.

Fig trees are considered sacred by followers of Buddhism, Hinduism, and Jainism. According to legend, Siddhartha Gautama was sitting under a sacred fig when he became enlightened, or "awakened." As a result, the tree is a popular symbol of happiness, prosperity, longevity, and good luck.

Two of the world's most famous sacred figs are the Bodhi Tree in India and the Sacred Jaya Sri Maha Bodhi in Sri Lanka. The Bodhi Tree is probably a clone descendant of the tree under which Siddhartha Gautama sat. It grows at the Maha-bodhi Temple in the state of Bihar in eastern India. Although its exact age is undetermined, it is considered to be most ancient. The Bodhi Tree performs a very important role for Buddhists of all traditions—as inspiration and a symbol of peace. For Buddhists, it is considered one of the most important holy sites in the world.

The Sacred Jaya Sri Maha Bodhi in Anuradhapura is believed to be one of the oldest surviving historical trees on record. English author H. G. Wells once wrote, "In Sri Lanka, there grows to this day, a tree, the oldest historical tree in the world which we know certainly to have been planted as a cutting from the Bodhi Tree in the year 245 B.C." This particular tree was brought to Sri Lanka by Theri Sangamitta, daughter of Emperor Asoka, and planted in the Mahameghavana Park in Anuradhapura by King Devanampiyatissa. It is said to be the southern branch of the tree in India under which Siddhartha Gautama attained enlightenment. Accurate records have documented that the Sacred Jaya Sri Maha Bodhi was planted in 249 B.C. (Wells was a little off). Every full moon of Poson, a festival in June, a million or so worshippers visit the tree to commemorate the introduction of Buddhism to Sri Lanka.

HUON PINE

2,500+ years

It's been used for furniture, cabinetry, and carving since the early 1800s. Oil from its wood (up to 7 percent of the weight of the wood is oil) is used as a paint preservative, for dressing wounds, for treating toothache, and as an insecticide. Its timber is resistant to rot and marine organisms, making it an excellent material for building boats. It is also highly prized for its golden yellow color and fine grain. With all this going for it, you might imagine that the huon pine would be in high demand. It is, and because of past logging and an unusually slow growth rate (about .039 inch per year), there are fewer than 26,000 acres of the tree remaining—all in the southwestern corner of Tasmania, the only place in the world where the tree grows. Luckily, these remaining stands are now protected within the Tasmanian Wilderness World Heritage Site.

Huon pines have been used for a variety of dendrochronological studies of long-term climate variation in the southern hemisphere. The trees are significant because of their extreme longevity. One sample collected in 1991 revealed a crossdated age of 1,089 years. Living trees sampled by increment borers have yielded ring-counted ages of up to 2,500 years. Some estimates of unsampled trees predict trees with ages in excess of 3,000 years (although this remains unverified).

Most huon pines are found in rainforest areas along river banks. The trees reproduce vegetatively, by layering and root suckering, as well as by seed. This plant is dioecious, meaning that male pollen and female seed cones are usually found on separate trees. The female cones are made up of fleshy scales, while the male cones are yellow and long. The seeds are dispersed by water. Most huon pines reach heights of between 32 and 65 feet, with some specimens topping out at 98 feet.

The pine's scientific name, *Lagarostrobes franklinii*, comes from two Greek words: *lagaros*, meaning "thin," and *strobes*, meaning "cone." The *franklinii* part honors Sir John Franklin (1786 to 1847), naval captain, arctic explorer, and governor of Tasmania from 1836 to 1843. He, unfortunately, did not live nearly as long as his namesake specimen.

GIANT SEQUOIA

3,266 years

The name giant sequoia is something of an understatement. These trees are truly the behemoths of the botanical world: The largest known tree on the planet—the giant sequoia named General Sherman, in Sequoia National Park—is almost 275 feet tall, has a girth of 109 feet, weighs an estimated 4,629,660 pounds, and has a total volume of 52,508 cubic feet of wood. That's enough wood to build more than a dozen 2,000-square-foot homes. "Giant" doesn't seem to do it justice.

Giant sequoias have long been known for their height. The tallest of the sequoias rise to the height of a twenty-six-story skyscraper. Their diameters at their bases exceed the width of many city streets. As they continue to grow, they produce about 40 cubic feet of wood each year, which is equal to the volume of a single 50-foot tree 1 foot in diameter.

Here are the heights of the five tallest trees, all in Sequoia National Park:

- General Sherman: 274.9 feet
- General Grant: 268.1 feet
- Lincoln: 255.8 feet
- Washington: 254.7 feet
- President: 240.9 feet

Giant sequoias also hold a record as one of the longest-lived tree species in the world. Crossdating of tree rings on cut stumps has shown that a sequoia in Converse Basin, at Giant

Sequoia National Monument—designated CBR26 by its discoverers—was at least 3,266 years old when it was felled (yes, it was cut down). Researchers have precisely crossdated 3,207 rings on the stump, and it was known that at least 59 years of the stump's sapwood was missing.

The age of the tree was determined using a complex formula that combines knowledge of tree size with information gained from partial increment cores. When tested on 231 sequoia stumps, this approach gave age estimates that were within 25 percent of the actual age 98 percent of the time, a level of precision substantially better than that of the previous method, which estimated tree age based on diameter alone. Using the newer formula, here are the estimated ages of select giant sequoias (again, all in Sequoia National Park):

- Cleveland: 2,890 years
- Washington: 2,880 years
- General Sherman: 1,650 years

The estimated ages of seven of the largest sequoias range from 1,650 years to 2,890 years, with an average of 2,230 years. Though all of these sequoias are much larger than CBR26, five have estimated ages at least 1,000 years younger. In fact, the largest living sequoia (General Sherman) is estimated to be little more than half as old as CBR26.

At 3,266 years, CBR26 makes the Giant Sequoia the third longest-lived nonclonal tree species known, exceeded only by two others . . .

ALERCE TREE

3,622 years

Southern Chile and the Patagonia region of Argentina are home to the long-lived alerce tree. Typically growing in temperate forests where there is a high seasonal rainfall, the tree (pronounced ah-LER-say) is a giant conifer related to the better-known giant sequoia and cypress.

Although pure stands can exist, the reddish-brown trunks of the alerce are usually seen emerging above a much denser forest of various broad-leaved trees. There, the trees wait for the competition to be eliminated before regenerating; for this species the elimination of competition is extremely intermittent and appears to be almost wholly dependent on destructive events, such as volcanic activity or fire.

Some scientists believe the alerce is better adapted to past climate conditions than it is to current ones. As a result, it is not competitive with modern tree species and is thus relegated to high altitudes and infertile or poorly drained soil. Even so, it can grow to heights of 165 or more and widths of 14 feet. It can also live for a long, long time: Through dendrochronology, at least one alerce sample has been estimated to have existed for 3,622 years.

The alerce is one of Chile's national symbols. Streets, schools, suburban housing developments, hotels, gas stations, taxi fleets, and a cell phone company have all been named after the "Sequoia of South America."

The species is in grave danger, however. Its wood is highly prized—tough and water-resistant and a much sought-after commodity for building construction (150-year-old alerce roof tiles are still in good condition) and furniture making.

Lumbering of the alerce in Chile began toward the end of the sixteenth century and continued unabated right up to 1976, when the species was finally declared a national monument and cutting was prohibited. The massive overexploitation had caused population numbers to decline dramatically; by the early 1900s, a third of the existing alerce forests had been lost. Even today, predatory cutting and burning have reduced its range by half. When sold overseas, the timber can fetch as much as five thousand dollars per cubic meter, thus creating a lucrative black market. It remains to be seen if this ancient tree will be able to withstand continuing threats from the modern world.

BLACK CORAL

4,000+ years

At around the time the stonework at Stonehenge was erected, between 2,550 and 1,600 B.C., an animal that is still alive today began its life on the floor of the Pacific Ocean near the Hawaiian Islands. Since then, civilizations have been built and have crumbled, cultures have risen and been eliminated, and continents have split and shifted. Using radiocarbon dating, researchers have learned that a unique species of black coral, *Leiopathes glaberrima*, has been alive for at least 4,000 years. To date, it is one of the longest living sea creatures known to science.

The age extremes of deep sea black coral make them critical "markers" in our efforts to understand the past. Many corals' skeletons grow in a manner similar to that of tree trunks, developing growth rings that become historical archives of water conditions over long periods of time. Analyzing the chemical composition of these layers allows researchers to trace changes in ocean circulation and temperature over hundreds or thousands of years. These historical records are critical in understanding how climate change occurred in the past and in making climate predictions for the future.

Radiocarbon dating of this coral has also provided marine biologists with valuable information about its long life, which is not easy. Fishing methods practiced by several countries, along with a lack of knowledge about coral in general, have led to extensive damage to these "Methuselahs of the Sea." As a result, while these slow-growing corals may be long-lived, they may also be in extreme danger simply because they cannot reproduce rapidly.

BRISTLECONE PINE

4,844 years

Walk through the soaring mountains of eastern California and you are likely to encounter one of the oldest living organisms on the planet: the bristlecone pine. These hardy plants live in an environment most of us would consider extreme, with a high altitude, cold temperatures, dry soils, and an extremely short growing season. Yet through it all, these amazing pines have survived, and even thrived.

Bristlecone pines are found throughout the western United States. They comprise three separate species: the Rocky Mountain bristlecone pine (in Colorado, New Mexico, and Arizona), the Great Basin bristlecone pine (in Utah, Nevada, and eastern California), and the foxtail pine (in California). Bristlecone pines typically grow—very slowly—in isolated groves at or just below the tree line. Bristlecone wood is very dense and resinous and thus resistant to invasion by insects, fungi, and other potential pests. As a tree ages, though, much of its vascular cambium layer—the layer that surrounds the roots, trunk, branches, and shoots, extending throughout a tree—often dies. In very old bristlecone pine specimens, this often leaves only a narrow strip of living tissue to connect the roots to a handful of live branches.

One of the oldest single living organisms known today is a bristlecone pine nicknamed Methuselah, located in the Ancient Bristlecone Pine Forest in California's White Mountains. It has been estimated through an analysis of core samples to be

4,739 years old. To protect it, the U.S. Forest Service has not revealed its precise location within the bristlecone pine grove.

In 1964, an even older bristlecone was discovered, when University of North Carolina student Donald Currey was taking core sample of bristlecones in eastern California. During the sampling process, he discovered a tree that was "clearly about 4,900 years old." When his coring tool broke, the forest service granted him permission to cut down the tree, nicknamed Prometheus. After the tree had been felled, 4,844 rings were counted on a cross-section of the tree. This made Prometheus the oldest living thing known to science at that time.

FUNGUS
8,500 years

I must admit that I am not a big fan of mushrooms. I don't like them, don't eat them, and seldom talk about them. And this is somewhat difficult since I live in Pennsylvania, which proudly celebrates the fact that mushrooms are its num-

ber-one cash crop. It is unbelievable to me that the world market for mushrooms is in excess of forty-five billion dollars a year. That seems like an awful lot of money to spend on fungi.

Even I was amazed, however, when I came upon an item in the *International Journal of Medicinal Mushrooms* reporting that there are approximately fourteen thousand species of mushrooms throughout the world.

I was also stunned to learn that in the Malheur National Forest in the Blue Mountains of eastern Oregon there lives what many scientists believe is the world's largest organism by area—and that it's a fungus known as *Amillaria ostoyae*. It seems this giant covers 2,384 acres, or 3.72 square miles. That's one humungous mushroom. (Here's another way to think about the size of this organism—imagine a mushroom that is 1,488 city blocks big.)

Just as amazing to me is that this organism is believed to be between 2,000 and 8,500 years old. While the thought of eating *any* mushroom sends chills down my spine, the thought of eating a fungus the size of 2,254 battleships that's been aged for more than eighty centuries is enough to make me eschew vegetarianism forever.

NORWAY SPRUCE

9,550 years

If trees can be considered tenacious, then there's one in the Dalarna province of Sweden that exemplifies the definition. This ancient Norway spruce first took root just after the end of the last Ice Age. When the tree was carbon-14 dated at a laboratory in Miami, it was discovered to be 9,550 years old. In the soil underneath the crown of the tree were another three generations of wood from the same clone, dating (respectively) 375, 5,660, and 9,000 years old, all with the same genetic makeup.

In the Swedish mountains, from Lapland in the north to Dalarna in the south, scientists have located clusters of Norway spruces that are more than 8,000 years old. These trees have survived harsh weather conditions because of their ability to push out another trunk whenever one dies. According to scientists, the clones take root each winter as snow pushes low-lying branches of the mother tree down to the ground. A new erect stem emerges, one that often loses contact with the mother tree over time. The trunks of the mother tree may only survive for about 600 years, but the tree itself is able to grow a new one.

Ten millennia ago, a spruce would have been extremely rare in this part of the world. It is quite possible that the ancient humans who lived in this region imported the tree, suggesting that humans immigrated close to the receding ice front. In support of this theory, scientists have found fossil acorns in the area, indicating that people may have taken the acorns with them as they migrated.

Norway spruces can give scientists valuable insights about climate change. Specifically, studies of these trees have proven to scientists that it was much warmer at the end of the Ice Age, and that the ice disappeared much earlier, than originally thought. This seems to suggest a pattern of climate change over the centuries that may add to our knowledge about the past and help predict the future.

The Norway spruces in Sweden probably survived so long because of the generally cold and dry climate in which they live, few forest fires, the ability to clone themselves, and the relatively sparse human population.

CREOSOTE BUSH

11,700 years

I f you wander around the deserts of the American Southwest, you will undoubtedly encounter many examples of the creosote bush. Distinguished in February through April by its twisted yellow petals, the creosote is a prominent feature of the desert landscape. It can be found in Nevada, Utah, California, Arizona, New Mexico, and parts of Texas.

The creosote is an exceptionally hardy evergreen shrub with waxy, pointed, yellow-green leaves. Its foliage provides refuge for desert grasshoppers, crickets, and praying mantises. During severe drought, a creosote bush might drop some of these leaves, but it never loses them all. A typical bush grows to about 4 feet in height, although specimens up to 12 feet are not uncommon. The plants are uniquely adapted to the harsh environment in which they live.

The creosote bush, often referred to as chaparral, is today marketed as an herbal remedy. It was used by Native Americans as a sunscreen as well as a potent antioxidant for the treatment of blood poisoning and hepatic diseases. Clinical studies have confirmed the potency of the creosote bush in treating these disorders. Research has also shown that compounds in the plant have been linked to a higher incidence of liver cancer in certain groups of humans. Exciting new data suggest, however, that extracts of the plant may inhibit the growth of various forms of cancer.

When a creosote bush is somewhere between 30 and 90 years old, its oldest branches die, and it sends up several new stems on the edges of its root crown. Eventually, the old root crown dies, leaving a ring of new, separate bushes, each one a clone of the original plant.

In April 1980, scientists discovered a clonal creosote colony (now known as the Ring of Creosote Bush) near Lucerne Valley, in the Mojave Desert. This semicircular colony had an average diameter of 45 feet. When it was carbon-dated by a scientist at the University of California, Riverside, it was shown to be 11,700 years old. Other equally old specimens are more than likely scattered throughout this remote region.

MONGARLOWE MALLEE

13,000 years

Also known as the Ice Age gum tree, mongarlowe mallee is one of the rarest trees in the world. To date, only five individual specimens have been discovered, all near Braidwood, in New South Wales, Australia. Scientists are still at work determining the exact age of a particular specimen estimated to be approximately 13,000 years old. In order to verify this, they are carefully examining the plant's growth patterns and overall growth rate. They are also performing a genetic analysis of nearby specimens to determine if they are from the same organism or are distinctive individuals.

If the five specimens are genetically identical, that means they all originated from a common root base. If this can be proved, then these plants may be part of the world's oldest living tree. Here's a way to think about this: In the 13,000 years since it sprouted, more than five hundred generations of humans have come and gone from the earth.

There is some speculation that the five isolated populations of mongarlowe mallee all are clones of long-vanished original trees that survived the last glacial period about 12,900 years ago. The trees are extremely hardy and tolerant of poor drainage, as are several other species of eucalyptus to which they are related. Equally important is that the seedlings of mongarlowe mallee often show evidence of hybridization with other species. That seems to indicate that the species itself (along with other eucalyptus species) may be of hybrid origin.

If you could look carefully at the small leaves of this amazing tree you would notice that they are the thickest of any eucalyptus. You would also see that they are studded with large oil glands, possibly an adaptation to deal with killing frosts. A close look would also reveal that the leaves are curved at the ends.

One of the most interesting discoveries associated with this tree is that the seeds have a very low viability; in short, the tree sets new seeds but produces few new seedlings. In the laboratory, the seeds have been artificially germinated only after having been placed in freezing temperatures for several months at a time. This leads botanists to speculate that current winters are not cold enough or long enough to promote germination. The last ice age in Australia, approximately thirteen centuries ago, may have been the last time temperatures were low enough to naturally germinate the seeds. The lack of cold (perhaps due to global warming) may be the death knell for this long-extant species. Indeed, current climatic conditions may be so significantly different from those in the past that we may see the end of several long-lived botanical species in our lifetimes.

BOX HUCKLEBERRY

13,000 years

Approximately thirteen thousand years ago, a comet measuring about 2½ miles in diameter exploded in the skies over what is now North America. Fragments of the comet were scattered over a large expanse of the region. Enormous conflagrations spread across the continent, destroying much of the vegetation that many animal species, specifically mammals, needed to survive. The death of those mammals would have had a significant effect on other species throughout the food chain. The ancient Clovis people, who inhabited North America at that time, would have lost a most valuable food source. It is certain that the comet's impact had a deleterious effect on this culture: It is perhaps the main reason the Clovis people died out.

Scientists at the University of California at Santa Barbara were able to piece together this possible sequence of events through an analysis of archeological sites at which there were high concentrations of iridium, a rare substance on earth, but a common element in comets and asteroids. When comets crash into the earth, they leave behind a blanket of iridium that can serve as a geological marker.

Also approximately thirteen thousand years ago, a box huckleberry seed germinated in what is now south-central Pennsylvania. Box huckleberry is a low shrub with creeping stems known as rhizomes that rise to about 1 foot high. New stems sprout from underground rhizomes to replace older,

dying branches in a continuous process of vegetative reproduction.

The box huckleberry has glossy, leathery leaves that lack the
resinous dots of other huckleberry species. And unlike other
huckleberries (which are deciduous), the box huckleberry
holds its leaves throughout the year. It has white or pink bell-
shaped flowers that produce fruit similar to blueberries but
with larger seeds. It blooms in May and early June.

Just north of Harrisburg, Pennsylvania, is one particular
box huckleberry that sprouted from that ancient germinated
seed. Measuring about a quarter of an acre in size, it's a single
specimen that continues to exist despite the encroachment of
industry, the spread of suburbia, and the persistent car exhaust
from nearby interstates. It has been alive for some 13,000
years, as extrapolated by its known average growth rate of 6
inches per year.

Whether this box huckleberry could survive another comet
crash remains to be seen.

SPONGE

15,000 years

I t's an animal with no brain, heart, or stomach. It can be smaller than your thumbnail or large enough for you to hide inside it. It can live in the warmest seas or the coldest oceans. And its life could be as short as a few months—or as long as several centuries. What is it? A simple sponge.

Many people think sponges are plants because they have the outward features of a large bush or small tree. Sponges come in a variety of shapes and sizes: fan-shaped like ferns; with tall, thin tubes like tropical flowers; with branches that extend in different directions, like many shrubs. Like plants, sponges come in many colors: Some are bright orange or red, others are deep blue or green (these colors come from algae living in the sponge's skin). But sponges are true animals. They catch and eat food, mate, take oxygen from the water, and make waste products. They don't, however, have the capacity to move from one place to another; they mostly cling to rocks.

There are approximately fifteen thousand species of sponges found throughout the world's oceans. Many can be found along coral reefs; others live deep underwater. Although most are saltwater creatures, there are about 150 species that live in fresh water.

In fact, sponges are some of the oldest animals on the planet. Many lived before the time of dinosaurs. Fossilized sponges dating to more than 580 million years ago have been reported.

What may be most remarkable about some sponges is their overall life span. It is well known that Antarctic sponges grow extremely slowly due to very low water temperatures. A single specimen growing in the Ross Sea near Antarctica has been scientifically estimated to be 15,000 years old. In examining this individual, scientists discovered an unbelievable number of growth rings. After ring counting, one scientist stated that the specimen "appears to be the longest-lived animal on earth."

KING'S LOMATIA
43,600 years

The year was 1934. A solitary tin miner named Charles Denison King was poking through the wilds of southwest Tasmania when he happened upon an unusual shrub with shiny, green leaves and pink flowers. Over the years, he kept an eye on the distinctive plant. In 1965, he sent a specimen to the Tasmanian Herbarium to be identified. Botanists discovered that the plant was actually a colony of plants, each one genetically identical to its parent.

The original plant that King discovered has since disappeared (and likely died out), but two similar clusters of approximately 500 plants cover an adjacent area of about 1,312 square yards. This is believed to be the sole remaining colony in the wild of the shrub known as King's lomatia.

King's lomatia has three sets of chromosomes (it's referred to as a triploid) and is therefore sterile. Reproduction occurs only vegetatively: When a branch falls, it grows new roots, establishing a new plant that's a clone of its parent. Often called King's holly, although it's unrelated to holly plants, the lomatia does not bear fruit or seeds.

Although all the plants in the Tasmanian colony are technically separate (each has its own root system), they are collectively considered to be one of the oldest living plant clones. Each individual plant's life span is approximately 300 years, but the plant has been cloning itself for at least 43,600 years. When this colony of plants began its life, Neanderthals were living across much of Europe, and mammoths and giant sloths were roaming North America. The estimate of the plant's age is based on radiocarbon dating of fossilized leaf fragments found in the vicinity of the colony that were identical to the contemporary plant in both cell structure and shape.

The area in which King's lomatia grows is prone to fires and other natural threats, such as root rot fungus. As a result, Tasmania has begun an effort to develop other populations in controlled environments such as the Royal Tasmanian Botanical Gardens. But doing so is difficult. Because of the plant's inability to reproduce sexually, scientists cannot increase its genetic diversity to promote disease resistance.

The Tasmanian devil, an aggressive, dog-sized creature distinguished by its hair-raising screeches and sharp teeth, is probably Tasmania's most famous wild citizen. Interestingly, the devil's life expectancy of 5 to 6 years is considerably less than that of the Tasmanian King's lomatia in which it sometimes hides.

QUAKING ASPEN
80,000 years

Located in Fishlake National Forest in south-central Utah is what might be the heaviest known organism in the world. Here a clonal colony of a single male quaking aspen has been growing for a *very* long time. Clonal colonies are not unusual. They are typically a group of genetically identical plants growing in one location that have all originated vegetatively from a single ancestor.

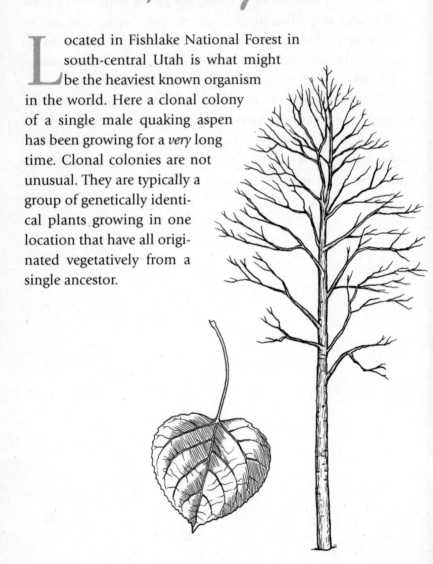

This particular aspen specimen has been named Pando (Latin for "I spread")—a reference, no doubt, to its underground root system that extends over 107 acres, the equivalent of some 47.5 city blocks. Every part of the plant has identical genetic markers, lending further evidence to the conclusion it is indeed a single organism.

Pando has been estimated to weigh about 6,615 tons (or 13,230,000 pounds, or the weight of 882 full-size school buses).

Much of Pando is a collection of some 47,000 root stems. This extensive system itself is called by some scientists one of the oldest known living organisms in existence—estimated at 80,000 years, based on when climatic conditions were last suitable for seedling germination.

SEA GRASS
100,000 years

Spread throughout the Mediterranean Sea, the species of sea grass known as *Posidonia oceanic* forms enormous underwater meadows. As its scientific name indicates, it is, like Poseidon, a god of the sea indeed. Found at depths of up to 100 feet, sea grass is a flowering plant with bright-green, ribbonlike leaves. It is sometimes known by its common nickname, Neptune grass. The foliage of the plant often forms balls of fibrous material that frequently wash up on shore. The large fruit of the plant is known in Italy as "the olive of the sea." Apparently Italians like their olives the size of volleyballs.

In 2006, a huge clonal colony of *Posidonia oceanica* was discovered south of Ibiza, an island in the Mediterranean about 50 miles from Spain. The colony, approximately 5 miles across, was estimated to have an age of some 100,000 years.

BACILLUS SPHAERICUS
40,000,000 years

In May 1995, a sample of *Bacillus sphaericus* was discovered by Raul Cano in the gut of an ancient bee that had been encased in amber. The rod-shaped bacteria looked just like millions of other kinds of bacteria in the world. From the bee's abdomen, Cano extracted several bacteria spores that were in a state of suspended animation. Those spores were reanimated in the laboratory. I don't know if Dr. Cano had ever seen *Jurassic Park*, but it is certain he was trying to do something other than converting this bacteria into a prehistoric beast.

For apiarists (bee scientists), these spores are important because they are a natural part of a bee's digestive function. For other scientists, the material was valuable as a toxin for a particular strain of mosquitoes—it has been used to reduce mosquito larval populations throughout the world.

But it wasn't the toxicity of the bacteria that was so interesting. It was its age: 40 million years. Now one might argue that a state of suspended animation is quite different than a life filled with regular cycles of respiration, digestion, and reproduction. Nevertheless, I think we can agree that the possibility of any other kind of 40-million-year-long life would be just this side of unbelievable. Although research is continuing . . .

BACILLUS PERMIANS
250,000,000 years

Headline: "Million-Year-Old Critters Living in New Mexico Caves." That may have been the front-page article in October 1999, when the 250-million-year-old bacteria *Bacillus permians* were found in ancient sea salt in Carlsbad, New Mexico. As was the bacteria *Bacillus sphaericus*, the microscopic *B. permians* organisms were reanimated in a laboratory after being in a state of suspended animation for several thousand centuries.

There is, however, a small cadre of scientists who doubt the authenticity of this specimen. They base their reservations on the fact that spores contain no active DNA repair enzymes—therefore, DNA tends to decay into small fragments. (This may be due in large measure to natural radiation in the soil.) As a result, this bacterium should have lost its viability within several hundred years, at most. And so, unfortunately, any estimation of the bacteria's age is tenuous at best, and most certainly challengeable.

Of course, *B. permians* will be subjected to further examination before definitive conclusions can be made as to its longevity. Stay tuned.

JELLYFISH
immortal?

The jellyfish has no skeleton, heart, eyes, or brain. Its body is 97 percent water, and its skin is as thin as tissue paper. This fragile creature seems like an animal destined to live a very short life. Yet jellyfish (as a group) have survived for more than 580 million years, far longer than any dinosaur.

Depending on the species (there are between twelve hundred and fifteen hundred), jellyfish life spans range from a few hours (in the case of microscopic *hydromedusae*) up to several months. The jellyfish that inhabit coastal waters typically have a life span of 2 to 6 months.

Most jellyfish species have tentacles that trail their bodies. These are lined with hundreds of stinging cells, each one filled with a small amount of toxin. The well-known Portuguese man-of-war has more than two thousand stinging cells per inch of tentacle. With scores of tentacles, it can have tens of millions of stingers.

Another jelly, the Arctic lion's mane, is probably the longest animal on earth. With tentacles reaching lengths of more than 100 hundred feet, it is longer than an adult blue whale, the largest animal in the world.

Most jellies pass through two distinct stages during their lives: the polyp stage, in which the tiny creatures live on the bottom of the ocean or drift on ocean currents, and the medusa stage, what we commonly recognize as a true jellyfish, with its characteristic body parts. Jellies in the second stage usually have a "bell," which some species use to float on the surface of the water. Other jellies are able to travel underwater by pumping water in and out of their bells. (To go long distances, most species, as they did during their polyp stage, generally hitch a ride on ocean currents.)

In one of the most startling biological discoveries in recent years, scientists in Italy report that a very small jellyfish, *Turritopsis nutricula*, found throughout the world's tropical oceans, has the ability to reverse its life cycle. Believe it or not, this allows the jellyfish to bypass death, rendering it biologically immortal.

How does *T. nutriculas* accomplish this feat? It can actually alter the differentiated state of a cell, transforming it into another cell type. This phenomenon, called transdifferentiation, is usually seen only when parts of an organ regenerate. It appears, however, that the process occurs normally in the *T. nutricula* life cycle. Through transdifferentiation, the jelly reverts back to the polyp stage after becoming sexually mature (and it can repeat this cycle indefinitely). This tiny jellyfish can *theoretically* live forever.

HYDRA
immortal?

I t's a flower that stings. It's a creature that eats its victims whole. It's an organism that somersaults across the floor of a pond. And it's named after the nine-headed sea snake of Greek mythology. What is it? It's a hydra.

Hydras can be found throughout the world, with about ten species living in the United States. Tan, gray, brown, or green in color, they are related to jellyfish, sea anemones, and corals.

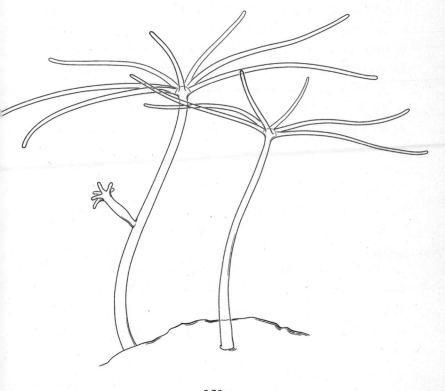

Green hydras get their color from algae that live in the cells of their body walls, which provide nourishment that allows hydras to survive for long periods of time between meals.

Hydras can be found growing on sticks, stones, or water plants in all types of fresh water. Shaped like thin cylinders, they are approximately $1/4$ to $1/2$ inch long. At first glance, they look more like flowers than animals. One end of a hydra is surrounded by five to seven tentacles that can stretch out to make the creature look like a long thread or pull back so it looks like an egg.

Hydras primarily use their tentacles to capture and eat small water creatures. Each tentacle has tiny cells that contain stinging threads. The threads are driven into an unsuspecting animal, and a poison is released that paralyzes it. The meal is slowly pulled into the hydra's mouth to be digested whole.

Although hydras usually stay in one place for long periods of time, they also "walk" across the bottom of a lake or pond. To do this, the hydra leans over and grips the surface with its tentacles. Then it somersaults into a new position.

Hydras reproduce through a process known as budding. From time to time, small knobs appear on the surface of a hydra. As the buds grow, they begin to develop tentacles. When completely developed, the new organism breaks off and begins its life as an independent creature. Hydras can regenerate and replace all their body cells in a period of several weeks.

Research conducted at the University of California, Irvine, suggests that the hydra is "capable of escaping aging by constantly renewing the tissues of its body." To test for aging in hydra, mortality and reproductive rates for three hydras were analyzed for a period of four years. The results were surprising, to say the least—*there was absolutely no evidence of aging in the creatures.*

It remains to be seen if signs of senescence—the deteriorative process that increases the probability of death with increasing chronological age—are observed in hydras older than 4 years. But there is already slight evidence suggesting that hydras may be ageless and, quite possibly, immortal.

One wonders whether creatures such as hydras and jellyfish—as simple as they appear on the surface—might know something that we humans do not.

POSTSCRIPT

At their best, statistics are tenuous. What may be accurate today will, most certainly, be less accurate tomorrow. Karl Popper, a philosopher of science, has affirmed that science proceeds not by proofs but by disproofs. In fact, new information is unearthed, new data are discovered, and new estimates are made all the time. Words like "approximately," "seemingly," "apparently," and "most likely" creep into scientific reports because research is never precise, never static. My biological colleague Dr. Karl Kleiner refers to these as "wiggle words"—words that scientists use to denote a hint of doubt in a body of research.

Nothing in science is ever 100 percent exact or certain. Everybody sees data through a different lens. There may be those who will challenge some of the figures, numbers, or statistics reported in these pages. That's okay by me. In several cases, trying to find a definitive answer to a question yielded a wide range of answers, with no two alike. Each scientist interprets data a little differently than do his or her colleagues, and each scientist uses statistics in ways that bolster his or her hypotheses, suppositions, and conjectures. Several scientists working on the same problem may all arrive at completely different conclusions. Some might say an organism lived for 3,600 years, others 3,622 years, and still others, "It appears to have lived for approximately 36 centuries." Which should I go with? Dunno.

Be assured, however, that every effort was made to verify the data presented here. Quite possibly, you may read other resources that contradict my figures, numbers, and statistics. That doesn't mean my information (or your information) is erroneous, only that it might have been interpreted differently or reported using a different set of criteria. That's just the nature of science. And that's why "wiggle words"

ACKNOWLEDGMENTS

This book was conceived shortly after I read an account of *Dolania americana*—a critter whose momentary life span (5 minutes) makes six-decade-old authors truly appreciate multi-vitamins, power walking, and any other current medical advances that extend human longevity. As I became absorbed in this topic, I realized how much I would need to tap into the expertise of others to verify my data and confirm my research. I would have to stand on the shoulders of scientists (a most uncomfortable position, to be sure) and tap into their expansive and professional expertise. For if it is true that no book is solely the work of the author whose name appears on the cover, then this book was graced by the contributions of many biologists, zoologists, botanists, and researchers whose life works echo across every page.

But there is one individual whose commitment and dedication to this project deserve special celebration and honor. Dr. Karl Kleiner is a biologist of extraordinary talents, uncommon skill, and intense perception. He took on the role of fact-checker with his usual good humor, precision, and scientific fervor. While juggling his own professional agenda, he tracked down facts, pursued isolated bits of data, and doggedly verified information at every turn and every juncture. This book is as much about his determination to ensure accuracy as it is about each of the featured species. He is the consummate scientist— one who passionately parses facts and carefully reaches conclusions that underscore the vitality of the scientific method. I am forever indebted to his professionalism, spirit, and service—this book would not have been possible without him. You, the reader, are the ultimate beneficiary of his erudition and persistence. I am the fortunate beneficiary of his friendship, authorial guidance, and camaraderie.

I am also deeply indebted to the Faculty Development Committee at York College of Pennsylvania for providing me with the necessary research funds that allowed this project to progress. Their review of the initial application and resultant enthusiastic support of this venture allowed me to conduct on-site research across the country, confer with some of the best biological minds around, and employ the fact-finding expertise of my friend Karl Kleiner. Their uncompromising support is fervently celebrated throughout every entry.

As ever, my wife Phyllis deserves the highest kudos of all. Early-morning typing, mid-afternoon research, and late-night editing were all endured with her usual support, encouragement, and love. She, too, was an eager supporter of this venture and a wonderful sounding board in my constant search for new information and equally compelling stories. And now that my authorial duties are over, Honey, I guess it's time for me to finally tackle that clutter we call a garage!